Juneau W

A Teenage Boy's Perspective on Life

Juneau Wang is a seventeen-year-old boy. He is a high school senior and loves art, music, food, and swimming. Juneau is inspired by both biology and the human connection shared between all. He has published a scientific article titled "Los abejorros: expertos en electricidad" in the March 2019 issue of *Albricias*, a national journal created by the American Association of Teachers of Spanish and Portuguese. He is certified to teach yoga mindfulness. Most importantly, Juneau continues to seek happiness.

A Teenage Boy's
Perspective on Life

A Teenage Boy's Perspective on Life

*Making the Most and
Finding Happiness*

JUNEAU WANG

ISBN: 1-6967-8177-9
ISBN 13: 978-1-6967-8177-0
Library of Congress Control Number: 2019916536
Slingerlands, NY

Author photograph © Courtney Sorbello
Book design by Juneau Wang

CONTENTS

ACKNOWLEDGMENTS

I AM UTTERLY BLESSED to have been able to write this book. I would like to thank all that the universe has given me. Most importantly, I would like to thank the amazing people who have guided me on my journey towards happiness. Every interaction has led me to this point and proven to me that life is beautiful.

First, I must thank my family. The support, acceptance, patience, and love that they give me every single day are things for which I am truly grateful. My love for them goes beyond words. I am honored to have grown up by them. I am grateful for the constant encouragement that I can reach for the stars. I thank them for raising me to become the young man that I am today.

Next, I would like to thank my teachers. From them, I learned life perspective that goes beyond class projects or unit tests. Ultimately, I learned what it means to be human. I remember their teachings and life stories. I cherish their ways. This book was not spontaneously generated—it was nurtured by the efforts of the teachers who wanted me to take what I learned and create for myself. I am honored to have been taught by them.

Acknowledgments

Finally, I thank my friends. There exists no better source of fun and smiles than from the people around me. I want to thank those who supported my ideas and endeavors all throughout the years. I would like to thank Thomas Buffaline, Mike Guyette, Maddie Kaplan, Trystan Melas, Joey Mocerine, Regan Murphy, Jerry Sweeney, Lia Soares, and Jason Wu for taking time out of their days to review my writing, give me advice, and encourage me to make this book even better. I am blessed to have you as my very good friends.

FOREWORD

I T'S BEEN THOUSANDS OF WORDS. Hundreds of hours. And after writing this book, I have come to one very important conclusion: *my life philosophy is a paradox*. However, my life perspective has been crucial to my journey towards happiness, and I hope it may help others, too. So, let me detail you my Paradox Theory.

There exists a constant theme of duality throughout my entire book. I spit out clear, concise ideals that are maybe contradictory and ask you to figure out what they mean to you. I do have one thing going for me, though—my words are the stones of my perspective, not the tenants of a universal solution. I simply hope that you may learn something from the definitions I've learned, the experiences I've faced, and the choices I've made. I want to help those around me.

My perspective is a version of the yin and yang. I believe there exists a lightness and a darkness within all of us. Although they may contradict and although they may fight, we can mindfully dedicate ourselves to ensure that the two components do not tear us apart, but rather fully develop our whole selves. This mindful dedication to accepting every aspect of ourselves and the world around us is the path towards happiness.

We'll start simple: doctors versus robots. When I was in Vietnam shadowing medical and surgical rotations, a medical student told me something very important: medical staff help people who are going through the worst days of their lives. Therefore, the people who work in a hospital must be extremely compassionate. While robots can write prescriptions and diagnose diseases with great accuracy, they cannot as of now help us when we break into tears. As human beings, we have the ability to emotionally understand one another. In Chapters 7 and 8, I investigate the ideas of compassion and sentiment. I explore society, respect, integrity, and how we should go about adversity, both daily and extreme. Why do people get offended? Can guys sing? Are we defined by the bad things that happen to us?

Next, truth and kindness, my two most important personal values. But these things can often go against each other. Should I be frank and say "I hate your outfit," or should I be kind and say "I love your outfit"? In Chapters 5 and 6, I establish something which I call the "positive truth." While both "seeing the glass half-empty" and "seeing the glass half-full" are technically correct, only one of them is the right way to look at life. I believe there is a way to both accept reality and also look at it from a wholeheartedly positive perspective. From such, a question arises: when do we say what we need to? And in Chapter 9, I push the boundaries of honesty and kindness. When do we speak up and tell the truth no matter what those around us say? What if the truth hurts someone?

Along with these values come juxtaposing beliefs. I believe it is our duty to fight for what we want, that our destiny is in our hands. But I also feel that coincidences happen, and random incidents occur from which we must learn. The publishing of this book is currently one week behind schedule, but that's not stopping me from publishing it. And additionally, things have coincidentally happened within this one lagging week that I have added to this book. I don't know if my failing schedule is meant to be, but I know that I can make the most of it and continue to fight for myself. Chapters 3 and 4 focus on actively improving our own day-to-day situation and gradually achieving independence.

In accordance with fighting for oneself, we must learn how to be both an unconditional self-lover and a proponent of the moral fiber. We should accept ourselves for who we are. But at the same time, we cannot accept immoral past actions. How do we forgive ourselves, love ourselves, and move on? In Chapter 1, we will discuss self-actualization, and how we can find passion and begin to accept the world. In Chapter 2, we will investigate what it means to love oneself. And in Chapter 4, we will explore the different stages of morality. I hope I can show you that you are unique, you are perfect despite your past mistakes, and we all must continue to improve ourselves and know by heart our own identities and values.

But I would be doing a disservice by writing a foreword just to summarize what I have already written. I want to make something clear: I am not yet the person that I aspire to be. In another contradiction, I consider my greatest accomplishment "happiness," and my most important goal for the future "happiness." I believe there are some things that we are never done with. There are important paths which we must actively walk that show us to our own existence.

I was blessed with the opportunity to work as an intern one summer at The Marshall Centre Helicobacter Research Laboratory at the University of Western Australia. My advisors were Doctor Alfred Chin Yen Tay and Nobel Laureate Doctor Barry Marshall. To say that I learned a lot from the Centre is an understatement. I ate lunch with coworkers. I experienced how real life goes on in a different country. I developed social skills, work ethic, a passion for medicine, and a knack for making automated scripts with Linux. But most importantly, I realized the strength of promise. On my last day before returning to America, Doctor Tay and I said one thing to each other: "we will see each other again." For some reason, I still think about that promise to this day. And I continue to remember my promise that I would visit Arirang Korean Barbecue in Perth one more time.

There are things that I cannot answer or explain. Life may take me away at any moment. But at the same time, I believe that our promises mean something. It's these promises that you feel not in your gut but in your heart. I realize it's another paradoxical path that I choose.

I know life may take me away at any moment. But I also know it won't; not because I can control what lives or dies, but because I made a promise to the universe. And that promise carries a weight heavier than its words or its feeling. It can be felt from underneath the ground and heard from above the clouds. That promise is the human commitment, the thing we so desperately hold onto despite the fragility of our lives. Despite the knowledge that we may leave at any day, we cannot stop fulfilling our destiny, because to the heavens we made a promise. Call me naïve, call me idealistic, but maybe those traits are not such a bad thing. No matter what pushes me down, I trust in my beliefs. I hope that you may trust in yours, too.

How can we be both truthful and kind? How can the world be both our oyster and a wild bull? How do we live knowing each day could be our last but continue to promise the universe from the bottom of our hearts? Why are we both rational robots and irrational, emotional humans? So, my theory is a paradox. But it doesn't stop me from living, loving, and finding happiness. I know that I'm not yet the person that I aspire to be. But I never give up.

Enough of this foreword. Let's start with the book.

A Teenage Boy's
Perspective on Life

CHAPTER 1

The Most Important Thing in Life

P AT YOURSELF ON THE BACK. Yes, *you*. Do it. Before I begin my spiel, I would like you to realize something about yourself: *you are a trooper*. You have travelled down every path imaginable—the good, the bad, the ugly. Not only that, you have conquered it all. You're alive and kicking, aren't you?

I want to be the first to congratulate you. Today you remain standing, victorious, having taken on every single day that has led to this day. So, pat yourself on the back.

This is already difficult enough to ask others to do. Simply put, people seem hesitant to congratulate themselves of anything. Instead of letting themselves feel proud, people throw away others' compliments. You might even have found my words sarcastic or ingenuine. You might have felt that you do not deserve such applause. You might have discarded my celebration of you as "pansy," weak, or stupid. Maybe you discredit me because I'm a teenager—how could I ever understand the difficulties of life? How could I understand all that you have been through? It is impossible.

You are right. I may not fully understand what you have been through. But the fact that you are still here means something. Just like how I am here—I like to believe that it means something. So, please take my congratulations. Take this positive energy and do not convert it into the negative. Bear with me and see if you, or someone you know, and I have something in common.

Hello, I'm Juneau. I'm 17 years old and have just started my senior year in high school. I am one of the 42 million teens in the United States, almost 13% of the population. I'm gonna be real—teens are the most misunderstood population. Adults don't understand teens. Kids don't understand teens. Teens don't even really understand teens. But here I am, a teenage boy, and here's what I have to say.

Before I jump into the details of my life, some details typical, some unique, please allow me to first clear up some (super-duper fun) foundational science and history which is crucial to the understanding of my perspectives. By the end of this book, no matter from what walk of life you come, whether you are a teenager like me, or you are a parent, sibling, teacher, or neighbor, I hope you will be able to take away something from this and look at teenagers and everyone around you with a new perspective. We are all finding our own ways through life.

From looking at the past, we begin to understand that our ancestors have struggled as much as we do, trying to figure out what life is and how to live a better life. I would like to discuss humanistic psychology (my favorite) and its predecessors. Humanistic psychology will then show us the hierarchy of human needs and, in my opinion, the most important thing in life.

To harness life's blessings is a lesson that resurged in the mid-20th century. World War II, nuclear warfare, and the Cold War proved that we, human beings, could obliterate ourselves in an instant. From the constant, looming threat of extinction came an ideological need to purposefully take full advantage of our short and fragile lives. Thus, in the field of psychology arose a "third force"—humanistic psychology.

Long story short, the first and second "forces" have depressing views on human nature. First, Freudian psychology states that we are all savage animals who struggle in controlling our desires. And according to Sigmund Freud, those who create great artistic achievements are simply products of abnormality.[1] The idea that we are uncontrollable animals who may succeed only because we are abnormal is not something many want to hear. Secondly, behavioral psychology states that animals (us included) do things simply because of external incentives and that we have no free will. Modern behavioral psychologist John B. Watson claimed that he could turn any infant into a doctor, a lawyer, or a thief, "regardless of his talents, penchants, tendencies, abilities, vocations, and race of his ancestors."[2] Later, behaviorist B.F. Skinner also attacked the usefulness of freedom and dignity in society. In other words, we have no choice and "resistance is futile." This is pretty depressing stuff.

In contrast to Freudian and behavioral psychology, psychologists Carl Rogers and Abraham Maslow rejected the previous focus on savage instincts and comparison of humans to animals. Influenced by Renaissance ideals, over decades they developed humanistic psychology. The humanistic approach focuses on the uniqueness of each individual, claiming that humans cannot simply be defined mechanically by animalistic instincts or by experiments done on lab rats. We have free will and judgment and are naturally good; those who are bad or flawed can at any time reconnect with their inner selves. One humanistic theory sheds light on what are the most important things in life and why we do the things we do: Maslow's hierarchy of needs.

According to Maslow, people have a natural desire to fulfill specific needs one-by-one from the most basic to the most individualized. They are (1) physiological needs, (2) safety needs, (3) love/belonging needs, (4) esteem needs, and (5) self-actualization.

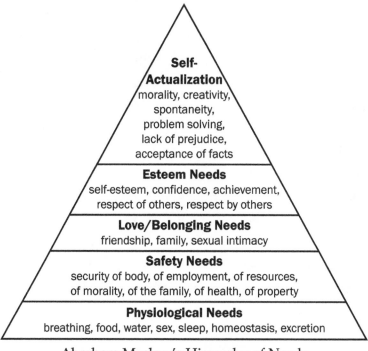

Abraham Maslow's Hierarchy of Needs

First, we humans have basic physiological needs such as food, water, warmth, and rest. Once those are fulfilled, we seek safety, such as with shelter from danger. Then we move on to psychological needs. We have an innate desire for intimate relationships and friendships, known as love/belonging needs. These pave the way for esteem needs, such as feelings of accomplishment, self-importance, and prestige. Finally, at the highest level, we strive to satisfy self-fulfillment needs with self-actualization. In other words, you would realize your talents, your full potential, and would find happiness in doing what you do.[4] For example, Doctor Holly Swanson, a successful medical doctor at the pediatrics center where I do my annual check-ups, has painted 10 of the exam rooms with bright and beautiful landscapes. These paintings have calming effects on the patients. Better yet, painting gives Dr. Swanson joy as well.

The hierarchy of needs has been viewed as an insightful model into human's motivations. However, there are many aspects that the hierarchy does not cover. First, achieving each level is not just a function of the person, but also of society. This can be seen today with the rise of millennials. Previous generations desire financial security and often find it imperative—a safety need. Millennials, on the other hand, desire leisure and experience much more. While having less financial security, they yet seem to be doing fine. For us teens, the new Generation Z values experience as well but also has stronger work ethics and values financial security more than millennials. Different "societies," either distinguished by location or time, can have different perceptions on human need.

Additionally, are our needs truly hierarchical? Many scientists and artists have starved themselves of physiological needs to achieve success in self-actualization. For example, Vincent van Gogh's *Bedroom in Arles* succinctly depicts the simple living conditions in which van Gogh lived as a "starving artist."[5] I'm not asking you to starve, but

The Most Important Thing in Life

I believe that needs are not strictly hierarchical, rather fillable "buckets" that vary in importance from person to person. For example, I vividly remember forgetting to eat lunches or dinners because I was engrossed in writing music or playing saxophone. Music has been an intense and bright source of happiness throughout my life that takes my mind and body soaring through the skies, waters, and mountains. Is what I feel self-actualization?

Vincent van Gogh: *Bedroom in Arles*. Collection of Musée d'Orsay, Paris.

Nonetheless, I believe self-actualization is an amazing objective. When one is self-actualized, they can create, develop their own sense of morality, be open and receptive to changes and new ideas, and accept facts or things for what they are. There is a famous quote that is often attributed to ancient Chinese philosopher Confucius: "Choose a job you love, and you will never have to work a day in your life." *To find pleasure in what you do is the goal.*

However, the goal itself is not the most important thing in life, but rather the correct motives behind it. Ultimately, self-actualization holds its strength in something more general but even greater: the pursuit of happiness. The United States Declaration of Independence declares that the pursuit of happiness is one of the "unalienable rights" of mankind. In addition, I believe that you can attain happiness no matter where you are on the hierarchy of needs. But don't get into the mindset that you simply deserve happiness without doing anything—you must get into the mindset that you deserve to *pursue* happiness. You must seek happiness out purposefully and work on it before you will "never have to work a day in your life."

But unfortunately, society doesn't help people pursue happiness. The stories that grab the most attention are the negative ones. The news outlets want to get the most views, and oftentimes the most advertising revenue, by discussing the terrors and horrors going on in society. While it is important that people be knowledgeable in all aspects of society, the ridiculous emphasis of bad makes people ignorant of the good. If you turn on the TV right now, would you be more likely to hear about a recent successful charity event or a supposed "unconstitutional atrocity" that a politician is committing? I understand that exposing the bad things in life helps encourage the improvement of society, but glossing over the better things in life makes the world bleak and dreary. This problem, however, is not only with the news.

While humans can and should socialize, too often do people talk about negative material. The good stuff is downplayed. Modesty, a good value by itself, for example, states that people should not speak "too much" of their achievements nor their successes. However, "modesty" becomes extremified and turns into "never talk about yourself in a good light, ever, or else you will make others jealous and annoyed and they will hate you." We consequently keep our positive energy to ourselves. So, what do we do instead? We talk about the bad things that have happened to us. Occasionally we truly need to confide in others, but sometimes it's simply for the attention and sympathy. And soon enough, these trivial negative stories take hold over our lives and mindsets. The traffic you experienced on your way to the restaurant should have no effect on how much you enjoy the food, but for some reason, it *does* have an effect. When we fixate on the negative past, it deprives our enjoyment of the present. Instead, we should learn to smile and laugh at the inconveniences of our past, not let them weigh down our shoulders.

When I was a child, my idol was not a scientist or an actor or a musician… it was Budai, an ancient Chinese monk and deity in many Buddhist sects. In the west he is often mistaken for Siddhartha Gautama, the Buddha himself, however Budai is different. Budai is considered the "Fat Buddha" or the "Laughing Buddha"[6] and is probably the smiling statue you would see in Chinese restaurants. I believe everyone has something to learn from his laughter.

I remember the stories my mom would tell me about him. I was chubby as a kid, and mom always said I looked cute, maybe as chubby as Budai. I would look in the mirror and stare. Soon a faded haze would wash over my reflection. A golden, smiling man, as chubby as I, would be staring back at me. He would grin his teeth and make a huge smile. When I think of Budai, I think of a man carrying all his possessions on his back, a man who travels the world with few articles yet a million possessions. I think of a man who gives all he sees a magical gift from his bag. I think of a man who attracts luck and fortune by radiating smiles and sunlight. I think of a man who smiles in the hardest times. I think of a man who knows of all emotions and chooses laughter. I think of a man who enjoys eating food. Budai is still my idol. I hope one day I may laugh as much as he.

Buddhist monk Budai. Collection of The Metropolitan Museum of Art, New York.

If I could only be remembered for one thing, I would want to be remembered for being happy. And I hope I can show others how the winding path even in winter may blossom. We will soon talk about self-love, healthy versus unhealthy comparison, toxic versus loving relationships, and most importantly, the pursuit of happiness. Here's a teenage boy's perspective on life.

CHAPTER 2

Self-Care and Self-Love

W HAT'S GOING ON, JUNEAU?"
       "So, I started having this cough a few weeks
       ago—"
"No, not about that! First, what's going on with you?
How's school, swimming, Saxophone?"

I was very ill for a few weeks of April 2019. Don't worry,
I did eventually get treatment, hahah. However, this
interaction still resonates with me. Doctor Michael P.
Looney, another amazing medical doctor at my local
pediatrics center, within two lines broke away my mind's
narrow focus and opened up my life perspective. *You are
more than just your cough.* There are so many things about
you that matter—your achievements, your goals, the things
you're proud of. As humanistic psychologist Maslow once
said, we are more than just a "bag of symptoms."[1]

Self-Care and Self-Love

Every morning we look at ourselves in the mirror. But what are we looking for when we stare at our reflection? We're more often than not looking for our own imperfections. We're looking for zits and bruises and stray hairs. But we go out into the world, interact with others, and we don't pay attention to their zits or bruises or stray hairs. Maybe we notice them, but we know that they don't define the person. We easily recognize how the people around us are so much more. The fact that my friend has a pimple doesn't mean I will begin to judge him or meticulously calculate some decreasing function as to why he would be "so much worse" due to a blemish. So, why do we stare at ourselves in the mirror with such a judgmental energy? If we all told our friends the same things we tell ourselves in the mirror, we wouldn't have any friends. So why is it so easy for us to be so critical of ourselves and often look at our symptoms, or the "bad" part of ourselves?

If I were to ask you, "Do you love yourself?" Most of you would stare at me as if I were asking some dumb question, and then most of you would say, "Yes?" So, answer my next few questions:

Do you love yourself when you accomplish something big? Do you love yourself when you are able to help someone else? Do you love yourself when you look great? Do you love yourself when you are motivated to work hard? If yes, let us continue:

Do you still love yourself when you fail to achieve something you really wanted? Do you still love yourself when you cannot help someone? Moreover, do you still love yourself when you hurt someone else's feelings?

Do you still love yourself when your hair is messy, or when you add a few pounds? Do you still love yourself when you don't have enough energy or motivation to do something that you know you should?

If you answered "yes" to all of these questions, then you, my friend, most likely have self-love. Your love of yourself is unconditional.

But for most of us, we tend to answer "yes" to only the first set of questions. This is conditional love. It is dependent upon the situation. We love ourselves only when we feel like we "deserve" it. And we seem to be our own, critical judge and jury. This is not self-love. This is a transaction.

Transactions are learned behaviors. It's like when we give a dog a treat for rolling over. We would give the dog a treat *if and only if* the dog rolled over. But now we turn to love. Love shouldn't be something given "if and only if," yet your conditional love of yourself might have been learned behavior. Maybe someone used love as a reward for you when you did something good. Maybe someone withdrew love from you when you did something that was considered bad or inappropriate. Consequently, love becomes a transaction in your mind. Love becomes something that you give yourself as a reward for good behavior and withdraw from yourself as a punishment for bad behavior. You become a master but also a slave by controlling yourself in this way.

I want to make it clear: this is not your fault. And I don't want you to blame others either, because the majority of us don't know any better. Besides, society has always inadvertently and amorally rewarded the fittest, which is part of human survival.

Nevertheless, this kind of conditioning has many consequences. It will be hard to undo your personal conditioning to come to truly love yourself. Additionally, your learned behavior could have become an outward expression that affects the way you treat others.

I want you to picture some people you may know who are "uptight" or "judgey." Sometimes they have a reason to be so. But most of the time, they seem and act judgmental of others because, in reality, *they are judgmental of themselves*. To be honest, it isn't their fault. Imagine the pressure put upon them from parents, from social norms, from values they've always held true.

Let's look at arrogance as an example. Arrogance is when one has or reveals an exaggerated sense of one's own importance or abilities. This often comes in the form of scoffing, shunned looks at "you idiots!" when you do something wrong. Mr. Arrogant asserts a pressure onto you to "stop being stupid" while showing an air of superiority. But don't end this train of thought so quickly with a hatred for him. Look deeper into who he is. He has always valued intelligence and excellence, both of which often lead to superiority or success in society. More than that, he probably is actually intelligent. For as long as he can remember, he has tried hard to achieve such values in which he believes. But why would he need to prove to others that he is intelligent in such a rash manner by condescending others? Because at times, perhaps he doesn't believe it himself. Maybe others deprived him of feeling confident. Maybe internally he's insecure and is taking it out in the wrong way. Maybe his parents were arrogant, pressuring him into being "toxically superior," and his upbringing permeates in his interactions with others. Qualities and actions don't just spontaneously generate, they are sourced from many causes. This is evident in evolution, history, and almost everything around us.

Analyzing Mr. Arrogant may be a simple task. However, he is a streamlined, simplified, fictional human being which I have created. It's easy for us to judge others. But are you able to look at yourself in the same way? More importantly, are you able to forgive yourself for your flaws? Would you be able to forgive Mr. Arrogant? The first step to NOT putting down others is NOT putting down yourself. Only when you love yourself, may you love others.

I understand this is a weird way to introduce a chapter titled "Self-Care and Self-Love." Fortunately or unfortunately, I will NOT be detailing proper diet, exercise, teeth whitening, or acne removal (please refer to your dietician, physical trainer, dentist/orthodontist, and dermatologist, respectively... or simply your general physician... or the Internet). However, hopefully I can show you the most fruitful form of self-care, the right attitude about the world around you, and self-love, the right attitude about yourself.

"You've gotta check your bag man; you could've lost something."

"I never even opened my bag!"

"What if somebody stole something?"

"I'm in a quiet museum exhibit. Alone."

"Maybe that's what they want you to think. Maybe you dropped something, and somebody stole it."

"I would've heard it if I dropped something."

"Maybe somebody knew you were gonna drop something and caught it before it landed."

"That doesn't even make any sense."

"Alien technology man. Just check your bag, goddamnit!"

"Jesus, okay."

"You should have five things—your wallet, your keys, your phone, your glasses case, and your water bottle."

"Okay, I see all five things."

"Your vision is lying to you, man. Your eyeballs are whack. Grab each of the five things."

"Okay, I felt all five things."

"What if you counted wrong, dude? Grab each thing again."

"Geez Louise… I felt all five things!"

"You'd hate yourself if you lost something and didn't realize it. That would suck. Grab each thing again."

"You're a pain in the ass. I felt ALL five things!"

"Good."

"You're a dickhead. Hey, that exhibit looks interesting. I'm gonna enter that room. I love impressionism!"

"You've gotta check your bag man, you could've lost something."

This is a conversation that used to frequently occur in my head. I had a lot of obsessive-compulsive tendencies when I was younger. I also had poor focus unless I was focused on these irrational and anxious thoughts, in which case I would *only* focus on these obsessions. I knew my worries were irrational, but I was unable to stop them. My worries were intrusive, persistent, unwanted. In fear of losing control, I would do irrational behaviors over and over again: checking, counting, cleaning… you name it.

I always want my car to be as clean as possible. So, when I spilled juice on the driver's seat, I washed the seat with soap and water three times over. Then I used ten alcohol wipes. Then I used set-in stain remover. Then I used air freshener and disinfectant, in case of any germs.

Before I went to bed, I would set my alarm for the next morning. Then I would stare at the ceiling and worry about whether or not I set my alarm. I would double-check that my alarm was set. Then I would stare at the ceiling and worry about whether or not I set my alarm. *Maybe I accidentally disabled my alarm when I went to check that it was enabled*, I would say to myself. Eventually I would become too tired to continue the cycle.

I never consulted a doctor about these thoughts, but they persisted in my mind for years. I would tell myself that I "would absolutely hate myself" if I lost something valuable, if I didn't wash my hands again, if I got a question wrong on my homework. A lot of people misconceive my desire for academic excellence as being due to pressure put on by my parents (and my race, but we'll get into that later). In fact, my academic excellence came from an internal fear of getting something wrong. I would absolutely hate myself if I got something wrong.

It was simple logic in my mind: if the teacher taught everything, then I should be able to remember everything. If the test matches what the teacher taught, then I should be able to answer everything on the test correctly. If I make a mistake, then the test no longer reflects my knowledge, but rather my inability to maintain control, so don't lose control. It was simple logic but terrifying and pressurizing. I believe the majority of students check their exams over once or maybe twice before handing them in. I used to check four times at a minimum.

Anyway, it was hard living like this. Sometimes I still have these obsessions and compulsions, but I have been able to control them. I understand what it's like to beat yourself up. I understand what it's like to feel helpless and "not good enough." The remedy is to be comfortable with yourself. But self-love is easier said than done.

First, we must accept ourselves for our flaws. Frequently do I see people who neglect or ignore their faults because their faults give them insecurity or fear. Reasonably so, our faults cause distaste in our mouths. But we cannot take care of our whole mind and body if we cannot acknowledge, accept and comfort our own mind and body. I am not ashamed of my obsessions and compulsions. They are a part of me, and I love myself for who I am. Can you identify your flaws and love yourself for them? Are you willing to embrace them in the direct sunlight, outside of the shadows of the night?

But how can we live with our flaws? We take the best from them and make ourselves stronger. I turn again to my own example in hopes that you may find similar ways to redirect negative energy into positive energy. My obsessions and compulsions taught me how to seek perfection, and while I no longer let them rouse my anxiety in school, they proved to me that I can and will work hard and to the best of my ability. By my own choice I will not settle for mediocrity. I can and will ace this exam if I put in high-quality effort. I also seldom make spelling mistakes, which is especially useful for school papers. I turned from worrying about things I can't control to dedicating myself to better the things that I can control. Some days I feel like I truly give it my all, I can feel it at the bottom of my heart; but yet I sometimes still turn out mediocre. No matter what happens, I must continue to accept that's who I am and get on with life with a smile on my face.

Secondly, we must pride ourselves in our accomplishments. Pragmatics, or the "etiquette" of conversation, states that we should be modest. Correct, we should not brag about our accomplishments or about how amazing we are. However, that does not mean we should reject compliments, yet we do that all the time. For example, somebody compliments your soccer or piano performance. Apparently, that person was genuinely impressed with your skills and wanted to tell you such. Rather than accepting the gift of kindness, you say:

"Oh, you're too kind to me! I actually messed up this and I wasn't happy with my performance."

Dude. Take the compliment. In my opinion, the pragmatics of both giving and accepting kindness is much more important than extremified modesty. *The second you say, "thank you," you'll become so much happier with yourself, and others will see it, too.* To receive positive energy from others is a blessing, so express gratitude and continue the positive energy. So, go treat yourself! You deserve to feel good about yourself!

Finally, to attain self-love, we must embrace the idea that we are unique. *You* are different. You stand out, and that is okay! Throughout my rough years of middle school and high school, I was reluctant to audition for and perform in musicals. Even though singing was and still is one of my biggest passions, I was not confident in my own voice, I felt like an outsider compared to the thespians and dancers around me, and I was afraid people would not perceive me as "masculine." And when I didn't believe in myself during my junior year of high school, my extremely talented saxophonist friend, Maddie Fitzgerald, was put up with my pusillanimity and forced me to send in an application for *Titanic: The Musical* the night before auditions. I owe her greatly for having seen potential in me when I didn't myself. Yes, I stood out. Yes, it was weird singing in front of friends and family who never knew I sang. But to hell with it. Once I began to love myself, it didn't matter that I stood out. I am who I am, and I love what I love. You are unique, too, and that is the most brilliant thing about you. So, don't let anything stop you from loving yourself.

One comedic quote which always stands out to me comes from the video game Portal 2. Cave Johnson, the founder of Aperture Science, always pushed the boundaries of scientific innovation, sometimes controversially.

Anyway, he said something that still sticks with me many years later: "Science isn't about WHY. It's about WHY NOT. Why is so much of our science dangerous? Why not marry safe science if you love it so much. In fact, why not invent a special safety door that won't hit you on the butt on the way out, because YOU are fired."[2] Don't play it too safe when discovering who you are. You deserve to be able to love yourself and pride yourself in your passions. My first question when given the opportunity to audition for *Titanic* should have been "Why not?" as opposed to "Why?" When you're comfortable with yourself, you'll be more willing to take on novel situations and experiences in the world around you.

Now, let us discuss self-care. I believe self-care is the process and ability to improve oneself in a healthy manner towards certain goals. I also believe that self-care cannot be easily attained without self-love. Goals created without self-love may be dangerous or inadequate towards your own needs.

One part of my obsessions and compulsions that has stuck with me is my stubborn ability to keep habits going. I used to make sure I checked my exam at least four times every time. It was a painful but consistent routine. However, I began to transition my "habit-stickler" quality to more constructive and more useful tasks. For example, I have been practicing and learning Spanish on Duolingo every night for over 3 years in addition to my classes.

Sometimes I lose my streak, which is a painful experience, especially when reminded by the relentless notifications in my email and on my phone. However, I forgive myself and I return to Duolingo. Even when I make mistakes or suffer temporary incompetence, I don't give up the mission.

Self-care is at its peak when you are able to improve yourself daily, one step at a time, with high-powered focus. This can be anything—learning a new language, practicing an instrument, eating healthier, or even brushing your teeth twice a day. I'm sure you have considered eating healthier, or exercising more, or practicing an important skill. But often, people never act upon their desires to better themselves. This is because we are afraid of two things: time and failure.

First, I often hear from those around me, "I'm so busy and I don't have any time so why bother trying to start." The majority of people do not have a correct mindset about time. As we all know, time is finite, and time therefore is valuable. However, we are only busy if we *believe* we are busy. Busy is a word with a negative connotation which suggests that we are at our near-maximum capacity for things we'd be able to do in a given day. Sometimes, this does actually happen. I vividly remember one Friday when I was the only family member home. In the morning, I made breakfast and lunch and dinner and bolted out of the door for school. Immediately after school, I drove for 30 minutes to perform a vocal solo for the judges at the New York State

School Music Association festival. I then drove back to my high school, eating a bacon sandwich with one hand and steering with the other, to barely make it in time for makeup and costumes for *Titanic*. We had an amazing opening performance that night. Looking back on that day, obviously I was a little stressed. But I don't remember the stress anymore. I only remember the thrill of performance, the blood rushing through my veins, the roar of the crowd in front of me. I remember the savory and seasoned aroma of the bacon sandwich after a long day. That's when I realized that, as long as we can find ways to enjoy what we are doing, we will never feel "busy." You must "love the game," like many sports coaches would say.

This mindfulness is something that changes your mindset completely. Doctor Ellen Langer, social psychologist and tenured professor at Harvard University, details the effects of bad mindsets in her book *Mindfulness*. Mindlessness starts in childhood and can affect you forever. The negative effects associated with being mindless can impact business and social relations. You start off feeling you "are too busy to do anything" or "have a lack of options." Soon, you may develop learned helplessness, or the complete ability to improve your situation yet with absolutely no motivation to do so.

An experimental study in Doctor Langer's book focuses on a group of women who spend their days cleaning houses, which is quite long and physically intensive work.

When asked if they exercised regularly, all said "no." The groups were then divided into an experimental group and a control group. The experimental was now asked to "think of the cleaning as an exercise, like going to the gym." The control group was simply instructed to go about their lives as usual. After an extended period of time, there were dramatic results. The ladies of the experimental group lost weight, and their blood pressures went down, and they reported better well-being. The control group showed no physical, biological or psychological benefits. To be mindful, we must emphasize process over outcome.[3] Enjoy the journey, if you will. If you believe something is a chore, then it is a chore. But if you can enjoy the process, or at least emphasize the journey, you will never feel busy again. The road trip can be just as fun as the destination!

Secondly, people are afraid of failure. We are afraid of disappointing others whom we admire. We believe that failures reflect a loss of our own being, as if that one relay race you lost therefore forever hexed you to *become* a "failure." But failure is one of the most important aspects of life. To have failed means that you have tried and you have lived. And in the long run, what matters is what you do *after* failure. If you learn to enjoy the journey, each failure becomes a milestone of gradual self-improvement.

My fear of failure when I was younger was extreme. I always imagined building a giant, LEGO skyscraper that pierced the clouds. I imagined the tower nearing the moon, the sun and the stars. However, as it got close to its peak, even a small gust of wind or an accidental step would cause the whole tower to topple, for the bricks to no longer contribute to something greater and instead remain just like that, a pile of bricks. This fear was exaggerated by my own obsessiveness for perfection, for I put in tremendous physical and mental effort into everything I do. I couldn't handle the fact that forces outside of my control or mistakes I have made could prematurely dissolve my hard work. But eventually, I realized that it happens. Shit happens, people! It's not a bad thing. It just is.

I remember losing my Duolingo streak after 206 days. I was especially angry. I wished I could change the past, fix my mistake. But the past is the past, and nobody can change that. I didn't quit Duolingo. I simply started again, building from the ground up.

Sometimes we do disappoint others, but that is okay. Yes, disappointing our mothers is obviously very tough, and we should seek to improve; but we are only human. Doing to the best of our ability is all we can do. Therefore, doing to the best of our ability is *everything* we can do. If those around you cannot forgive you for a failure after you have truly tried your hardest, then perhaps they are not the right people to be around you. So, don't worry about failure. As my yogi, Bari Koral, once told me, "worrying is praying for something bad to happen." Go out there and do something! You will not regret having tried to improve yourself, but you will regret not having tried in the first place.

Another thing that I wish to emphasize is that you can start improving yourself any day. We often are afraid of change and afraid of putting in effort to try something new. To justify our unwillingness, we say "oh, it's too late" or "I've never tried before, so why bother trying now?" It's never too late to learn a language or a new skill. It's never too late to earn a degree. It is always better late than never.

My favorite example of "better late than never" is writing a diary. I started writing a diary in the middle of eighth grade. I am so proud to say that I've still continued writing every single day for over three years. I have every memory of my high school to look back on. I always tell those around me that they should start writing a diary, but very rarely do I see them try. They think that it takes up too much time, that other things are more worth it, that it's "too late now." Perhaps there are other things that are "more worth it," but the belief of such causes them to view themselves as busy and unable to start a diary. They automatically downplay their self-efficacy in fear of time and failure. Of course, writing a diary is challenging in the beginning, but even after two weeks it becomes an extremely healthy habit. The only reason I would ever be able to write a book on discovering happiness is because I have written down my experiences and emotions, both good and bad. Writing down my feelings allows me to better understand who I am as a person and how others are different in their desires, perspectives, and personalities. It made me more constructive, empathetic, and understanding. Not only that, some memories are hilarious looking back on, such as the day that I accidentally bought alcohol (more on that later in the book). Anyway, I encourage you to write a diary in whatever way you can. Please, at least try! I promise you that *your story is worth being written down*. Someone out there will need to hear it.

Your story can assist you in dealing with the world around you. I have become mindful, and in general my memory has also improved. This allowed me to become better with dates. As someone with a low attention span, I began to remember friends' birthdays, chronological order of events, and when specific incidents happen in my life. Moreover, I became more aware of the passage of time, which allowed me to appreciate each individual day. I also improved in remembering names. I had the astonishing opportunity to shadow surgical and medical rotations at Hue University of Medicine and Pharmacy in Vietnam thanks to FutureDocs Abroad. When I was there, I changed into scrubs, a hair net, and a face mask before watching a total gastrectomy. Inside the operating room I met two medical students from France. Due to all of our monotonous, sanitary outfits, I only knew them by their eyes and voices. I'm sure we all never expected to see each other in the same operating room again. However, a week later, I recognized what I could of their faces and voices and called out their names when I met them at a different surgical rotation. Honestly, I probably startled them, but they then chatted with me and complimented me for remembering people so well. I believe that writing a diary can help you know yourself and recognize those around you in much more details. Often times these details become the unique characteristics of life around you. In the end, the textbook that has taught me the most is my own diary.

We all have something to learn from each and every experience, no matter the outcome. We must focus on the journey. I know that bad things happen, and bad things suck. But we can't deny the bad. We can't ignore what we dislike. We can't destroy our past mistakes. Some of my worst experiences (which I will talk about later) led to my more profound understanding of life. And we are especially hesitant to learn from something when we are the party at fault. People are afraid of being wrong and deny ever being wrong because such threatens our existence, our self-image, our ego. But denial of mistakes prevents us from finding solutions for self-improvement. You must recognize your faults, forgive yourself for it, and then work hard to be better next time.

Continuing on the discussion of the ego, one aspect of Freudian psychology that is still relevant to this day (and apparent) is the defense mechanisms of the ego. There are many problems with Freud's original theory, including his consistent overemphasis of extreme, sexual desire and his lack of scientific evidence, but his ideas are still thought-provoking, and ego defense mechanisms can be found in most people. According to Freud, our psyche is composed of three parts: the id, the ego, and the superego.

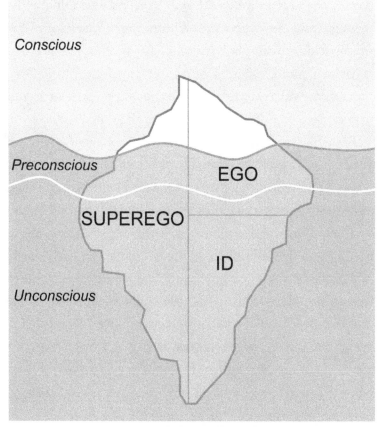

Iceberg Metaphor of the Freudian Psyche

The id is the pleasure principle, the "selfish being" which loves self-gratifying impulses.[4] The superego is the morality principle, the "selfless soul" which prefers others-oriented and self-denying demands. Too much id leads to selfishness and immaturity while too much superego leads to guilt and shame and self-doubt. The ego is the reality principle, the middleman, which balances the entire self with the real world. The id is entirely within the unconscious mind while the ego and superego are within the unconscious, the preconscious (can be consciously recalled), and the conscious mind.[5] This is often explained by the iceberg metaphor, which represents conscious, preconscious, and unconscious as different levels of depth in the "water."

So, what are defense mechanisms? They are the ways in which we shield ourselves from anxiety, guilt, or "unacceptable feelings" when we feel threatened or when our id or superego becomes taxing. While Sigmund Freud first noted defense mechanisms, it was his daughter, Anna Freud, who fleshed out these ideas. Denial, for example, is when one refuses to accept reality and unconsciously hides intense situations from awareness. I may refuse to recognize that I've improved less and less at swimming over the years. We often would rather ignore and run away from our sources of pain than confront them or try to make our lives better. Rationalization is when one cognitively distorts reality or the apparent truth to make a situation less scary or less uncomfortable. For example, If I don't get an interview for a job I originally wanted, maybe I'll say, "I didn't want that job, anyway." Displacement (my absolute least favorite) is where one takes out his or her anger on someone else.[6] These are just a few examples of defense mechanisms, and I'm sure we have all done one or the other. Defense mechanisms are natural and operate at the unconscious level to make the individual feel better, but that doesn't necessarily mean that the individual *is* any better. To become better, we gotta be truthful and we gotta learn, and most defense mechanisms avoid the whole "uncomfortable truth," let alone "learning." One of the best ways to deal with the uncomfortable truth is to focus on mindful understanding.

After each conversation, I try to contemplate how I could've spoken kindlier, more eloquently, and more attentively. Sometimes I say the wrong things in conversations, or accidentally cause offense. I feel pretty bad about messing up, but I don't let myself deny or rationalize or displace my guilt or shame. If you want to improve yourself and make yourself a better person towards others, you will always be mindful with every interaction.

Now that we have talked about time and failure as two of the biggest hurdles for one to try something new or different, I want to emphasize that sometimes we truly are busy. Although I advocate that you turn "busy" into "mindful enjoyment of the journey," what if your day is literally filled? Can you truly add another task on top of your busy schedule? Absolutely, if you are creative. Here, you can bring self-actualization into a whole new level. I will give you a few examples: my mother turns hair drying in the morning into a yoga practice. If she's jumping and twisting and twirling in the mornings while the hair dryer is blasting, don't freak out. My brother plays the drums as part of his cross-training for his arms and shoulders for swimming. When I am alone in the car, I shout and make loud and weird sounds to improve and increase my vocal range.

Now, I'd like to discuss a few final points for self-love and self-care. First, smile! Secondly, make clear exactly what you want. Thirdly, *don't be an onion*.

Smiling is something we should all do more of. Backed by both current research and common sense, smiling is contagious.[7] I know that perhaps the people you pass on the street aren't smiling, but that doesn't mean you can't. You have the ability to help brighten up a room. Why not do it? Smiling also releases neurotransmitters that make you feel good: serotonin regulates anxiety and heals wounds, endorphins relieve stress and pain, and dopamine is associated with the body's reward system.[8] Smiling is essentially our natural pain reliever, blood pressure regulator, and mood lifter.

Additionally, smiling makes others perceive us as more attractive. Researchers at the Face Research Laboratory at the University of Aberdeen, Scotland asked subjects to rate smiling and attractiveness. Both men and women were more attracted to images of people who smiled and made eye contact.[9] Ultimately, when you smile, people treat you differently. You come off as genuine, relaxed, and reliable.[10] I believe that putting positive energy into the world will bring positive energy back to you.

Along with smiling, people will find you genuine if you show others your wants and expectations. As a chubby kid in my youth, a lot of my friends' parents loved to offer me food—mashed potatoes, mac and cheese, watermelon, you name it. When I was younger, I used to think I was being polite by saying "no thank you" even if I really wanted those scrumptious-looking pancakes. But as I grew up, I realized that sometimes the most polite thing to say is to say exactly what you want. Accept those kind gestures. From my experience, parents (especially mothers) are so much more delighted if you allow them to indulge you in delicious food. And along the way, I learned that I really like turkey meatballs.

In addition to turkey meatballs, we should also make our own boundaries clear. I'm not saying that we should build humongous walls and show them off and isolate ourselves with our own boundaries—we should just kindly state what we would like ourselves and others to do. We should not offer more than we can give nor expect others to offer more than they can give. It is a wonderful thing to look out for others, but we should not literally break our own backs. When we trust that we will always be there for ourselves, first, and they will always be there for themselves, first, then the relationships we build among us will bring only positive energy.

Now, about being an onion… don't. You may not realize it, but you probably are an onion. Actually, we probably are all onions. In the movie *Shrek*, Lord Faarquad on the threat of death sends Shrek and Donkey to rescue Princess Fiona from the Dragon for Lord Faarquad in exchange for returning the swamp back to Shrek. On the way to the Dragon's Keep, Donkey questions why Shrek accepted the death threat and suicide mission rather than simply attacking Lord Faarquad with his brute strength and forcing him to return the swamp. Donkey takes the assumption from all previous interactions with Shrek that he is a violent monster who gets what he wants by means of aggression. However, there is more to Shrek than simply a savage beast:

> SHREK. For your information, there's a lot more to ogres than people think.
>
> DONKEY. Example?
>
> SHREK. Example? Okay, um, ogres are like onions.
>
> DONKEY. They stink?
>
> SHREK. Yes—No!
>
> DONKEY. They make you cry?
>
> SHREK. No!
>
> DONKEY. You leave them in the sun, they get all brown, start sproutin' little white hairs.
>
> SHREK. No! Layers! Onions have layers. Ogres have

layers! Onions have layers. You get it? We both have layers.[11]

There is more to people than meets the eye. What Donkey doesn't realize is that, ultimately, Shrek doesn't want to fight for peace. He doesn't want to resist anything as long as he can have his home back. Shrek is more than a green, giant ogre, he is a person with his own emotions and motivations, too. But Donkey's ignorance (in this case) is not his fault. Shrek has always hidden his softer side from the outside world. Due to his unique appearance, humans see Shrek and are immediately repulsed or terrified. The lack of love or positive energy given towards him causes his struggle with identity. People have always judged Shrek by his looks, and Shrek's behaviors begin to match their fears. So, Shrek begins to believe that perhaps he is just a green, giant ogre.

While one may easily discard this story as a computer-animated fairytale movie, I believe there is a great deal of emotional depth. Again, I do not believe that personalities or actions arise without cause. In this case, I find a parallel from Shrek to the social learning theory of reciprocal determinism. Before reciprocal determinism, behaviorist psychologists, such as Skinner, believed that personality is simply composed of behaviors. That is, external reinforcements strengthen some of your behaviors, and punishments weaken other behaviors, therefore creating your entire personality. You are nothing but reinforced and punished behaviors. If that sounds way too simplistic to you, another psychologist would agree with you as well. The behaviorist theory's one-way approach neglected the influence of the person on the environment. So, Alfred Bandura, with a novel social-cognitive perspective of psychology, developed the theory of reciprocal determinism, where your behavior, your personal factors (such as cognition and biology), and the environment around you all affect each other.[12]

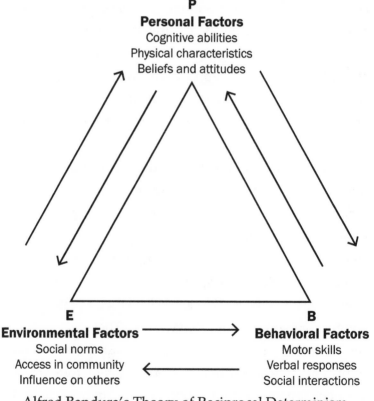

Alfred Bandura's Theory of Reciprocal Determinism

Self-Care and Self-Love

In the opening of the movie, Shrek's appearance (personal factors) causes the people around him (the environment) to be repulsed. The people collect pitchforks and torches and seek to attack Shrek. Shrek, valuing solitude (personal factors), changes from a relaxed behavior to one where he portrays himself as an evil, scary monster (behavior) to scare away the people (the environment).

Anyway, thank you for listening to my tangent on Albert Bandura and Shrek. What I'm trying to get at is that there exists a genuine "you"—one unhindered by the pressures of society and liberated from the self-imposed restrictions from your own cognition. Shrek at the end becomes a human with a personality, respecting love and friendship, much more than the monster that people regarded him previously. However, vanity rules his fantasy world as much as it does our world. The majority of people will not try to understand why you act the way you do; they will simply judge you. Often, this causes us to form layers. We wear masks to pretend that we are happy, or we are strong, or anything else valued in society. We don't want to stick out, so we hide our uniqueness under many layers.

What I want to tell you is that society therefore is constantly oppressive. Society is not bad, but its oppression is something to consciously look out for. Society is necessary to regulate people to an extent but is not here to totally suppress. Going back to Freudian theory, I believe that society emphasizes the superego and outcasts the id.

They want us to often self-deny and infrequently self-reward. But we need a perfect balance to keep our ego sane.

Show your uniqueness. Don't be afraid to go against the grain. Don't be afraid to go for what you want. You don't need to wear a mask or ten layers. You don't need to hide the true "you." The strongest people are okay with accepting the truth. The strongest people are okay with helping themselves as well as others.

And so, in conclusion, don't be an onion.

CHAPTER 3

Academics, Athletics, and the Arts

A FTER GRADUATING from the University of Neuchâtel in Switzerland, a young, bright man walked the streets of Paris seeking opportunity. He began to teach at the Grange-Aux-Belles Street School for Boys. While working there, he helped create and administer intelligence tests in cooperation with the headmaster, Alfred Binet. But when giving the tests to the boys of different ages and looking at the results, he noticed something peculiar. The younger children seemed to consistently give wrong answers to specific types of questions, no matter the intelligence or "individual quotient," as future tests following its path would be called. This man, Jean Piaget, did not focus on the fact that the children's answers were wrong. Instead, he created a theory to explain the phenomenon—the cognitive processes of a child are constantly developing and naturally different from those of adults.[1] His ideas may sound simple to us, but they would soon have profound impacts on the future of education.

To Jean Piaget, learning is very individualized. Children do not behave or think like miniature adults. They are "active builders of knowledge—little scientists who construct their own theories of the world."[2] That is, children do not passively absorb knowledge like a dumb sponge, rather, they actively seek and create mental models that explain their individualized universe. All new knowledge is filtered purposefully through pre-existing knowledge, where children must either assimilate new things into existing schema or "accommodate"—modifying old or creating new schemata—to fit new things. As children, we seek to have our schemata match reality. And through four basic stages, we build a new view of our own universe.

First, from birth to two years of age, we undergo the sensorimotor stage. We start off as tiny, cute, chubby babies who only have reflexes (like grasping and sucking... think about why these would be useful!). Then, we begin to develop new habits from accidental actions. Eventually, we begin to interact with objects around us, again, usually by accident. But squeezing the squeaky toy sounds funny! So, we'll keep squeezing it! We eventually get the idea that we can do other things with the squeaky toy… what happens if we throw it? What happens if we push it off the table (other than our parents getting angry)? And by the end of the stage, we develop object permanence, or the understanding that objects continue to exist even when we cannot see them. Babies who still love peek-a-boo have not yet developed object permanence, which is why they giggle or are startled when you reveal your face.

The second stage is the preoperational stage, from two to seven years of age. Now, we're pretty cool. We can mentally represent and refer to real-world things with words and pictures. We can also play pretend! However, we cannot understand others' perspectives or simultaneously think about multiple different characteristics of objects. For example, if I wanted a LEGO set for Christmas (hahah, I actually want a LEGO set…) but Sally wanted a racecar, and someone asked what I thought Sally wanted for Christmas, I'd say, "LEGOs!" If I wanted LEGOs, obviously Sally would too, right? Another example would be if someone poured a glass of water into a wide glass and then poured all the volume from the wide glass into a tall glass. I would say that the taller glass has more water because the water is taller. I would fail to consider volume and how liquids have definite volume but no definite shape. Eventually, we realize that other people think differently. This allows for things like deceit, empathy, and social interaction.

From seven to twelve years of age is the concrete operational stage. Now we develop total mastery of mental operations involving what is, but not yet what is possible.

The final stage is the formal operational stage, where we can finally do abstract thinking and systematically examine and test hypotheses.[3]

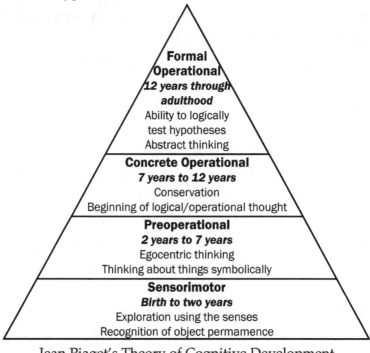

Jean Piaget's Theory of Cognitive Development

As you can see, I've grown tired of creating my own informational diagrams and have resorted to using the same triangle over and over again. Anyway, the main idea is as children, we actively seek knowledge. We have a childlike curiosity. But there are a few problems in the real world. First of all, as a teenager with many close peers, it seems that the "childlike curiosity" is beaten out of us after 12 years. Secondly, some adults are still egocentric. And finally, not all adults reach the formal-operational stage.

I wouldn't be the first to claim that the majority of educational systems around the world value grades more than knowledge. I also wouldn't be the first to claim that athletics and the arts should be just as valued as academics. But I want to show you how you can succeed, not only in the limelight of public attention but also, more importantly, in self-fulfillment.

As you know, I used to be quite the anal person. Probably still am, slightly. Thankfully, I've learned how to appreciate and chillax more when I'm at school. Overall, I am mostly internally driven when it comes to achievement. Such started early on with my obsessions and compulsions but soon transitioned into a simple desire to do the best that I could, not worrying about the outcome as much if I truly knew I had given my best. However, there is one main external factor that also keeps me motivated to work hard, so we'll start with that:

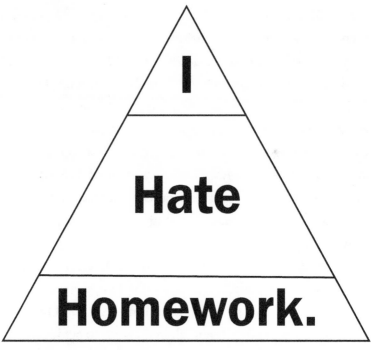

Juneau Wang's Theory of Hating Homework

There. I even made a nice triangle informational diagram. One of my biggest reasons for success was my hatred of homework. Now, forgive me for using the word "hate" because it's a negative word, but such is necessary to prove my point. Let's not think about the classroom just yet... let's simply consider homework. I do not foster a dislike of many things. It is potentially unhealthy to foster a constant dislike of something because you should stay open and spend your time focusing on positive things instead. However, dislike can be both logically reasoned and healthily dealt with. I believe this is a good example.

Yes, I am fully aware that constant reinforcement of information is necessary for effective memory retention. I'll even talk about memorization later. However, I never liked homework. Why does my mother get to work at Rensselaer Polytechnic Institute, come home, make a few business calls, and then watch TV and write her book for the rest of the night? In fact, the main thing that burdened me from writing this book is homework. There are so many things that I wish I could do instead. Freshman year, it was playing video games. I liked Overwatch a lot. Sophomore year, it was staying after school to hang out with my friends and talk to girls. Junior year, it was Minecraft, and also my book. Anyway, what I realized is that homework is a necessary evil, and it can be dealt with in extremely effective ways.

We must think abstractly for this (get ready for some formal operational stuff!). Imagine that quality of dedication towards work is the independent variable and that time consumed is the dependent variable. We'll measure "quality of dedication towards work" in Wangs, a number that ranges from 0 to 100, equivalent to the percentage of effort. If my effort is 95%, then my quality of dedication towards work is 95 Wangs. The more effort, and the higher quality of dedication that I put in towards my work means that I'll finish my homework in less time. For example, if I'm listening to music and talking on FaceTime and Snapchatting while I'm doing my biology homework, it'll take me around an hour. On the other hand, if I'm completely focused and dedicated towards finishing my biology homework, it'll take me 15 to 30 minutes. As the number of Wangs increases, the time consumed decreases... an inverse relationship.

The inverse relationship between quality of dedication and time consumed forever changed my philosophy about school and work. Any minute I had free during school where I didn't feel tired or stressed, I would intensely work on homework due the next day. I would finish quickly at home, and then spend the rest of my day 100% dedicated to the things I wanted to do (Overwatch, Minecraft, writing, music, et cetera). I could destress during these more enjoyable activities for me. I could fully appreciate them without the burden of homework hanging over my head. This also is the reason that I proudly claim that I am NOT a multitasker. When I listen to music, I only do just that. When I do homework, I only do just that. When I play Minecraft, I only do just that. Such is also an example of mindfulness. Too often do we try to multitask and eventually look back on low-effort projects that we have already forgotten about. We are not computers. I believe that putting your full heart into one thing at a time brings so much more yield, be it internal or external, than doing multiple things at the same time.

This approach allowed me to manage my time better and helped me realize that I can genuinely do so much in a given amount of time. If I don't *believe* I am busy, then I am not busy. However, one must take caution with this approach. First, you cannot let your work become sloppy. Secondly, this method only works when you are truly dedicated to it and truly hate homework. Saying "eh, homework is okay, not the best, I guess," will waste your time. And if you actually enjoy homework, then that is a blessing you should continue to cherish and you should not listen to me.

Now, I converted my hatred for homework into a mindfulness practice of dedication and effort. I didn't want school to seep into other aspects of my life, so I worked hard to isolate these aspects and made sure they remained pure goodness. This is good and all, but we also need to be mindful and dedicated in class.

I often hear from friends that they are disappointed in their results after having put so much time into something, be it academics or athletics or the arts. I get it, sometimes we feel like our hard work goes unrewarded. It does happen and it feels unfair. But that shouldn't cause us to give up or regret having put work in; we need to instead look to the future and find ways to improve the current situation. To do such, we need to look inward.

A man named Hermann Ebbinghaus conducted an experiment on himself. He learned a list of gibberish, 3-letter syllables until perfect recollection (like MUT, WOL, KOJ). Then, he would write down how many he remembered after an hour, a day, and so on until he could no longer recall any syllable. This serves as the basis of the forgetting curve. Forgetting happens quickly within the first hour and then tapers off gradually, and memory is better retained with distributed practice.[4] That is, it is better for you to review your schoolwork a little bit every day for a few weeks than it is for you to cram all the information the night before a test.

The Forgetting Curve

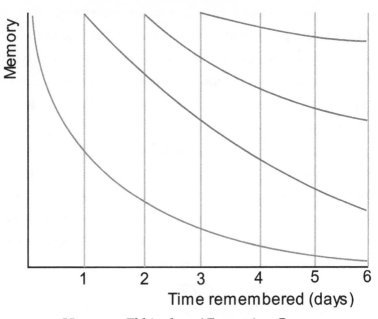

Hermann Ebbinghaus' Forgetting Curve

As a teenager, I know that the majority of students don't review schoolwork every day. Honestly, I don't think I could convince anyone to do that. But hopefully I can share with you a few tips which helped me remember school topics.

First, something I found more effective than distributed review after school was actually paying attention and listening actively *during* class. Way too easily do I see friends of mine zone out or get distracted. Hell, sometimes I play games on my laptop. But during times where the teacher is actually teaching, keep paying attention. Put your heart and dedication into learning with the teacher in that direct moment. You need to be paying so much attention that you notice when the teacher makes a mistake or accidentally slips up. You gotta live in the moment. Again, mindfulness. If you're not living in the moment, then school is just a waste of your time and you'll learn nothing. We can't spend our lives wasting it.

Secondly, we gotta be open. Classes are where we learn about new things which perhaps don't fit into our pre-existing mental models or schemata. But that doesn't mean we should just shut the teacher out and give up. We need to be willing to adapt and take on new content. Developing learned helplessness is not healthy, yet the majority of students experience it at one time or another. Sometimes it is genuinely due to poor teaching, but usually it is because students do not want to put in the effort to understand something they don't. Also, we should be confident enough to ask questions. If anyone judges us for asking a question, then it's their problem. Nothing should prevent you from seeking your best education in the moment.

Thirdly, actively find methods of studying that will help you understand and remember. Three non-intensive ways that have helped me include visualization, absurdity, and real-world application. When reading textbooks, we subconsciously remember where we learned what on each page. For example, I remember learning about the genetic bases of multiple diseases, and that it started in the middle of a page and at the top of the next page with type 1 diabetes. Often, we disregard this subconsciously remembered "mind-map" when we get to the test, but it actually can help quite a bit, whether it be with textbooks, note packets, or even videos. For my Advanced Placement United States History (APUSH) class, I did not read the textbook and instead paid attention in class and watched the Jocz Productions APUSH Reviewed series (shoutout to Mr. Daniel Jocz for the amazing videos!). Along with listening to my great teacher, Mr. David Rounds, who also tells brilliant and hilarious personal stories, and looking at his lecture outlines, I found my studying sufficient. I had encoded the information both visually with the videos and aurally with my teacher's lecture. Obviously, not all courses have free YouTube videos to help you but try to find what works for you the best.

I think often students study the way that their teachers want them to, which causes them to not even try to find better methods of studying. When I was taking global history my freshman year, I actually enjoyed reading the textbook but most certainly did not want to carry it around all the time. With some simple snooping around, I found an online PDF of an updated edition of the textbook that I could read on my phone! There are many ways to save time and create a better study environment, you just gotta look for them.

Finally, my last quick tip is that we should all open our minds to the idea that things can be pretty neat. Being judgey and close-minded is not conducive to growth. When Mr. Athlete makes fun of Mr. Bookie for being a "nerd," it is simply because Mr. Athlete has either been raised with different values (and lack of respect and perspective) or is insecure because he is bad at academics and therefore antagonizes academics in his mind in order to defend his ego. When Mrs. Popular makes fun of Mrs. Theater, perhaps Mrs. Popular really wants to sing on stage but simply doesn't have the confidence in herself (known as reaction formation). To be honest, anything is cool. Don't hate, be open to what others value. However, I understand why people try to act "dumb" to be "cool": they are afraid of others disliking them for valuing intelligence. I get that, and I've had my fair share of people dislike me for liking academic stuff. But that doesn't stop me from loving academic stuff. The people around me can say what they want. You are unique as much as I. So, love what you love and respect what others love.

When I say respect what others love, I mean from a healthy distance. We shouldn't concern ourselves too much with the doings of others. In order to succeed, we need to be a bit more "selfish." We need to focus on ourselves. First, you must develop an internal locus of control with an open mind. Your achievements are yours, no one else's. And accidents or failures are things you learn from and know you can improve in the future. My varsity swim coach showed me a quote by David Brooks: "Almost every successful person begins with two beliefs: the future can be better than the present, and I have the power to make it so."

We must be self-confident and self-assured in our ability to improve ourselves and know that our self-efficacy and self-esteem can deservingly grow. We must also learn to congratulate others on their achievements without a jealous eye and comfort others during their failures without condescending, judgmental pity. It is so easy to see everyone else's successes and feel bad about yourself. It is in our innate nature to compare. But what do YOU have? What can you bring to the table? A quote that rings with me is one attributed to President Teddy Roosevelt: "Comparison is the thief of joy." But I also believe it is *slightly* incorrect. Unhealthy comparison will destroy our desires to improve. Healthy comparison will show us what we admire and augment our dedication towards better.

When an adrenaline rush arises, when we have to perform, whether it be in front of a crowd, or adjudicators, or for a class, we all want to do our best. However, for years and years in attempting to do our bests, we end up with unhealthy habits. We lose sleep over exam preparation. We work and work without realizing the stress we put on our bodies, pushing our boundaries way too much in one sitting. When stress becomes paramount, we feel as if we're gonna fail the second we push off the block or pick up the pencil no matter what and end up performing terribly. Preparing for a performance is a tough task that requires the right mindset. When we work, we have to work smart, not hard.

First, the majority of hardworking America undervalues sleep even though it is one of the necessities. Sleep catalyzes a powerful restoration of both energy and matter within the body. And so, sleep deprivation can affect your mood, memory, health, and judgement. Sleep deprivation leads to higher levels of ghrelin, the hunger hormone, and lower levels of leptin, the appetite-control hormone. Therefore, lack of sleep makes us hungry, and soon we begin to eat junk food out of impulse. Our fatty cravings after a sleep-deprived night lead to eating too much starches, sugars, and salts. Consequently, there is a 50% increase in risk for obesity and a 48% increase in risk for heart disease according to Dr. Patrick Finan, a researcher at Johns Hopkins. Your immune system becomes compromised, and with the stress you're probably feeling throughout the day, you are three times more likely to catch a cold. Your body *needs* sleep time to recuperate your internal defense system. Without recovery time, you pile on more and more stress that has not only physical consequences but also mental and emotional consequences. You can become depressed, irritable, antisocial, anxious, and forgetful. Finally, surveys state that 1 in 25 adults have fallen asleep at the wheel in the past month, and that 6,000 fatal car crashes are caused by drowsy driving each year.[5] Imagine the potential of the students of America if only they could get enough sleep. Imagine the better decisions we would make, imagine the smarter answers on our tests thanks to our refreshed and healthy minds. Imagine the lives that would be saved.

I used to work on homework and study until 2:00-3:00AM. I like to consider myself a dedicated student, but the most disciplined thing I've ever done was realizing that *sleep matters more*. Once you view sleep not simply as an "option," but as a *necessity*, you will become a happier person. Adapting your workload in the beginning will be difficult, but you will learn to work around and cooperate with the fact that sleep is a must. And yet again, you will realize that you can do so much in a small amount of time. Do your best, but don't lose too much sleep over it.

Secondly, even in the hours when you are awake, *know your limits*. Humans are not biologically designed for the stress caused by worrying about and studying for an SAT for a month straight. We were meant to quickly run away from stressful situations or fight them directly... escaping or attacking a pack of wolves was meant to be done in a few hours, maybe a few minutes if you lose. Then, hopefully, we had a few days to recover before coming into contact with another dangerous threat. Becoming accustomed to consistent and potent stress in the school and work worlds is most certainly damaging to the body. Because stress biologically meant running away or fighting a pack of wolves, the body wanted to halt other functions, such as the immune system, so that you could spend most of your energy running or fighting. Now imagine being stressed for days on end. Immune-suppressing molecules, such as catecholamines and opioids, are released following stress. And studies show that there is an inverse relationship between plasma norepinephrine, secreted during fight-or-flight scenarios, and the immune function of white blood cells such as phagocytes and lymphocytes.[6] Simply put, the persistent stressors of society directly compromise your health and well-being.

Unfortunately, it is very hard to avoid stress in the school world. The three major times that I was sick during my junior year were April 2019, May 2019, and June 2019. April was the school musical and music festival performances for judges at NYSSMA. May was four Advanced Placement exams. June was the SAT. To top it all off, I had to drive myself to all of those because my mom had to care for my brother and her work. It kinda sucked being sick for those tests, but oh well. I did my best. I'm still navigating this "know my limits" path. I'm not there yet, but I know that I can get there. If you are unable to relax or stop at your limits, know that, although it is an unfortunate event, it *will* make you stronger in the long run.

Sometimes, training academically or athletically or even artistically can cause pain. "No pain, no gain," is a common saying; however, I feel it emphasizes the idea of pain too much. For example, weight loss does not require benching 300 pounds above your threshold or shooting yourself in the foot. We shouldn't be seeking pain, even if it is sometimes a side effect of improvement. Rather, I always remember a quote from Kung Fu Panda 3, said by Master Shifu: "If you only do what you can, you will never be more than you are now."[7] In conclusion, we should know our limits, and know that our limit is just above what we can do now. We can always grow.

Thirdly and finally, sometimes in performance we get too anxious and then perform poorly. So, I would like to talk about arousal. Not *that* kind. I know I'm a teenage boy, but I want to talk about scientific arousal, specifically optimal arousal. The Hebbian version of the Yerkes-Dodson law, often incorrectly cited as the original, is an empirical law which proposes that the relationship between arousal and performance is a bell curve for all tasks. The original Yerkes-Dodson law proposed that optimal performance for difficult tasks occurs at a medium amount of arousal, where interest and attention are adequate without tense anxiety.

For easy tasks, performance remained optimal at high arousal.[8] However, Donald Olding Hebb disagreed, saying that too much arousal would still decrease performance on an easy task,[9] thus arising the Hebbian Yerkes-Dodson law we know today.

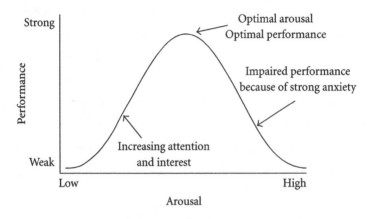

The Hebbian version of the Yerkes-Dodson Law

It is a generic law, but it also makes a lot of sense. It applies to tests, races, sports games, music performances, and even everyday life. If you're not paying enough attention, you could burn your food or break a lightbulb. Additionally, I believe that the law ties into my earlier statement about how worrying is praying for something bad to happen. If too much arousal, and therefore strong anxiety, causes decreased performance, then it almost seems like a self-fulfilling prophecy in its own right. Therefore, we shouldn't freak out about failing. Focus on staying calm and doing well and showing how good you are.

During my freshman year, I qualified for the Eastern Zone Short Course Championships in swimming. This was a competition between top swimmers in each district in the northeast. It would be my first Zones alone—my parents did not join me because my grandfather had passed away a few weeks earlier. This year I only had one event, the 400 Individual Medley, on the first day. The 400 IM is considered one of the most painful due to its use of all four strokes (butterfly, backstroke, breaststroke, freestyle) and its long distance. I qualified because I am a long-distance swimmer who doesn't complain about long distances, and I was good enough, but not the best in each individual stroke. Anyway, the team bus drove across New York and arrived at the hotel and swimming pool the afternoon before the first day. We took the time to get used to the pool and warm up. When getting on the block to do a start, I accidentally jabbed my knee into a little bolt on the side of the block (the diving block had just been redesigned to the new American regulations but was also dangerously implemented). I didn't think much of it, but when I got to the other end, I saw a gaping cut in my kneecap, an inch long and half an inch deep. I panicked and tried to stop the bleeding in the locker room. I shouted for my friend to get a lifeguard. That night was my first night in urgent care. I had six stitches and was panicking. Would I be able to swim? God, I prayed. I prayed to everything above. And a blessing came upon me—I was cleared to swim. It would be painful, and I had to make sure the wound didn't get infected, but I could swim.

I would insert a diagram here, but I don't think anyone wants my wound... distributed. Anyway, the next morning I peeled off my bandage and put on tegaderm. I warmed up before prelims; parents and coaches were freaking out. I probably should have been freaking out, too. But I wasn't bleeding, so I considered myself fine. No expectations. I just had to do my best. And the adrenaline hid the pain. I was afraid I would rip my stitches during breaststroke but went for it anyway. I am thankful beyond words to have had qualified for finals. And then the night came. One more time, except now, the crowds were paying close attention. Teams were playing close attention. This was finals. Get hyped up. I knew people were looking at my knee. I knew my team was worried I would bleed or something. But I didn't think about my knee. I just put my heart and sweat and (metaphorical) blood and tears into the race. I was in the lead for the first half but slowing down slightly during the breaststroke. Unfortunately, the man next to me passed me in the last 50 yards of the freestyle. But I got second place and a best time. It was my best placing ever at the Eastern Zones. I also didn't rip open my wound!

All you can do is put your all into it. You put in all your attention and heart and leave out unnecessary worry or anxiety. You let the heavens know that you want to do your best. I don't mean to get spiritual, but I think the above was looking down on me and protecting me. I was still thinking about the passing of my grandfather at this time. I believe he was protecting me. I hoped he could see me. And when miracles happen, I know he is with me.

CHAPTER 4

Independence

I BELIEVE WE ALL UNDERSTAND THE CONCEPT. However, from our different and unique walks of life, we all have a different perspective on it. In some places it is highly idealized, and in other places it holds negative connotations. So, what does "independence" mean? According to the Merriam-Webster dictionary, independence is:

> **in·de·pen·dence** \ ˌin-də-ˈpen-dən(t)s \ *n.* the quality or state of being independent[1]

Okay, great. That really cleared things up. Anyway, I would like to emphasize a few different uses of the word "independent" which I believe are the most important towards seeking a better life and addressing how to achieve independence. Here are the two "critical" definitions of "independent":

> **in·de·pen·dent** \ ˌin-də-ˈpen-dənt \ *adj.* not requiring
> or relying on something else : not contingent
> **in·de·pen·dent** \ ˌin-də-ˈpen-dənt \ *adj.* showing a
> desire for freedom[2]

I am a teenager. I live at home. On my parents' tax forms, I am a dependent. So how am I going to achieve independence, or at least continue to develop independence?

My journey may be similar or drastically different from yours. But all of our journeys towards independence will involve trial and error, adjustments, negotiations, even tugs of war with your surroundings. Our discovery of independence involves our interactions with our family, our teachers, friends, and others in society with whom we work. Please allow me to share with you a few examples, through which you might find methods to adopt or pitfalls to avoid.

First, food. You see, I started swimming at age eight. Practice was from 6:00-800PM almost every weekday. My mom would leave work at 5 pm, pick me up from after school care around 5:30PM, hand me an Ensure nutrition shake to drink in the car, and drop me off at the pool. God, I hated Ensure. But I did always get a light dinner after practice.

I soon took matters into my own hands. You see, food is very important to me. An Ensure was just not cutting it. So I decided that instead of always going to afterschool, I could take the school bus and get home earlier on the days that I would go to swim practice, which had been negotiated down to 3 times a week.

As a chubby eight-year old boy who loved all kinds of food but with no cooking skills, I experimented with all kinds of microwavables—Hot Pockets, frozen dinners, Jimmy Dean egg bowls and biscuits, and some very surprisingly yummy Lean Cuisine paninis and flatbread sandwiches. Thanks to America's frozen food industry that caters to busy work and family life, I started to delight in the variety of choices. This also allowed me to take control of, or at least have a say in, household grocery shopping.

Every Sunday morning before then, I pushed the cart behind my mom and waited for her to browse the isles and put food into it. As soon as I started to cook for myself, I started to have a say in what to get. But it was not that simple. As a "certified financial planner," mom managed normal household spending. So, she immediately challenged me to stick to a budget of $125 which was our usual weekly food cost. Suddenly, I was not only in charge of my own cooking, but also in charge of family meal planning and budgeting. I must tell you that it was not easy for a nine-year-old at the time; I had to lobby for several increases in the budget and also realized that better tasting microwaved foods were both more expensive and (probably) less healthy. However, I was able to argue that the time savings and the variety made the cost worthwhile.

I eventually learned to read the fine print of pre-prepared food and assess its "healthiness" by ingredients, cooking methods, and nutritional facts. I became increasingly mindful of what I put into my body and why, as well as the economic factors associated with it. This practice, from managing food, to managing money, to maintaining health, was very empowering.

Secondly, clothing. Teenagers really think about fashion. We each have a certain style that we are proud of; we each try to dress our best according to our similar or unique situations—for school, concerts, formal days, ball games, outdoor activities and parties. Yes, our lives are so full of activities, but our clothing needs can easily go overboard, or underboard, if you don't pay attention.

I believe in always presenting your best in all situations. *Your* best, not someone else's best. This is *not* a contest. It is about knowing what you want and abiding by what you need. I personally like high quality and high-tech stuff. Versace and Gucci of course would be amazing, but they're not in my budget (and their crazier products not in my fashion). Online shopping may sometimes be a curse, but I always methodically research the online reviews of the clothing and tech that I like and then determine if a product is worthwhile for purchase. As much as I love impulse buying, I try mindfully buy things that will benefit me in some way. I like to dress according to the occasion, but we often find ourselves with many different occasions. If we are mindful, we can develop our own personal style or clothing items that can be shared between many different occasions.

What goes in hand with clothing is laundry. If you do your own laundry, you will become much more sensitive about what materials or fibers you wear. Clothing affects the time, effort, and money that you put into laundry, folding, and ironing. Do you have time trying to prevent your cotton shirt from shrinking? Do you have time to do many different laundry loads? Do you have the money to pay others to figure this out for you? If you do, great. But if not, you should make sure you know what you'll be wearing (and cleaning) if you ever live on your own.

Finally, transportation. Transportation is a need that all people have that will continue to contribute to our independence or the lack thereof. As kids and teenagers, our parents shlepted us around for years and years for all our activities. My mom joked that she was my limousine driver. And when my younger brother started to need as much chauffeuring, she had to work out deals with other parents.

If you are not yet able to get a car or license (driving oneself is a huge sense of independence in America), you may not have much of a choice. But treasure what you have right now—bikes, buses, trains, Ubers. Soon enough we may be able to obtain the blessing, the freedom, and the responsibilities, of driving ourselves.

Part of growing up is to learn how to self care and how to manage daily living, including managing time and budget. But there is a substantial learning curve when it comes to the psychological aspect of independence. All the physical aspects of independence, whether aforementioned or not, contribute significantly to your psychological aspects. However they are not enough. There are several extremely necessary prerequisites for psychological independence. In order to pursue healthy independence, we need to be truly self-confident and self-aware human beings.

First, self-confidence is a journey, not simply a destination, that requires an immense amount of dedication and strength. To believe in yourself and trust in yourself is something that can only happen when you put down your foot and determine that you can do it. We always see around us people who are desperate to show others their knowledge, their personal expenses, and their lifestyles in desire for social approval. I used to be one of them. I would correct my friends' grammar to endless proportions. If you know someone like that, you know that they make you feel less about yourself. Those "people who talk too much" are craving validation from society by putting down others because they have no self-confidence in themselves. Unfortunately, this becomes a vicious cycle where true self-confidence is nowhere to be found, and everyone has to one-up everyone else in order to feel special. In this environment, it becomes hard to source an inner love for yourself. However, there are some extremely healthy habits and mindsets that can help boost self-confidence.

Doctor Carol Dweck noticed an interesting pattern while teaching at universities. She realized that students often had two different attitudes on failure—some students rebounded after poor performances while others were completely devastated by even the smallest mishaps. Eventually, she conducted many studies and coined two terms: fixed mindset and growth mindset, which sought to describe the underlying attitudes that people have about learning. Fixed mindset people believe that intelligence is fixed. Growth mindset people believe that, if they put in effort, they become stronger and smarter, often leading to higher achievement.[3] Fixed mindset people can be as successful as growth mindset people but are also more prone to giving up and are more insecure about their level of intelligence. I believe that the growth mindset can be applied not only to intelligence but also to self-improvement in general. In terms of self-confidence, it's not about where you are now—it's about the belief that you can grow if you put in the effort.

In addition, Carol Dweck challenges the main theory that a person's "willpower" is depletable and requires glucose. Rather, our willpower is only depletable if we think it is. She believes that people who have more abundant beliefs about willpower are less burdened by concerns such as "am I tired?" or "am I hungry?" and feel that they have more internal "resources."[4] I remember my best moments in swimming, my days of performance after performance, and my struggle to love myself. I would like to attest to the fact that believing willpower is infinite empowers you and allows you to do so much. I before mentioned that you are only busy if you believe you are busy. While time is finite, willpower is infinite. This idea greatly helps us boost our self-efficacy and our desires to make the most of every second.

Many other habits to boost self-confidence require control and mindfulness. One example is simply paying attention. If you want to stand up for yourself, you need to be attentive in the moment. You cannot argue for your point of view at a business meeting if you weren't even paying attention to the discussion. The idea that others know more than us can cause an immediate drop in self-confidence. Yet you must maintain the right mindset and control so as not to dwell in the dip, but rather work to improve both knowledge and self-confidence, and continue to be collected and constantly mindful. Take these opportunities to learn and grow.

Another example is decision-making. Making your own decisions gives you heightened control, and if you're mindful of why you made those decisions (i.e. "this is the option that benefits me the most without hurting anyone"), you'll be all the more self-assured. And you will live with each decision with ease and without self-doubt.

Finally, listen well and speak well. An ability to openly listen and respect the ideas and beliefs of others without judgment enables us to not only accept ourselves, but others as well. Earlier, I criticized those who speak of their achievements in a "desperate" way, as they often create a negative-energy vacuum to temporarily satisfy their need for validation. I believe there is a healthy and positive alternative which we can all achieve that ends with a simple clause: "and I'm proud of myself." To hear that sentence is psychologically rewarding to both parties. Simply declaring your own pride to someone else makes you feel even more confident in yourself; and the recipient subconsciously understands that you're not desperately seeking their approval or showing superiority, rather you're simply sharing a positive aspect of your life. In society, people don't often hear others say that they are proud of themselves; and that statement releases positive energy into the atmosphere and shows people that it's okay to love yourself. In conclusion, self-confidence is boosted by control, mindfulness, and positivity.

To be healthily independent, one must not only be self-confident, but self-aware. To me, self-aware means understanding your own situation, developing your own sense of identity, values, desires, and beliefs, and understanding how you are different from others. Most importantly, we must understand that it is completely fine if we are different from others.

High school teenagers have different levels of self-awareness. I sometimes talk to bright, amazing, and high-achieving students around me with one fatal flaw: they have no idea who they are. I become anxious and worried and distraught just thinking about it. I wish I could show all of my peers that they don't need to know what they want to do in 20 years, they don't even need to know where they'll be in five, but they need to know what they want right this instant. However, I've found that, to be completely honest, a lot of people don't want to be self-aware or independent. They don't even want to know what they want from life. Mindlessness can be a drug that relieves you from facing the sometimes-painful reality.

An aspect of our idealized society is delayed gratification. Corporate society emphasizes envisioning ourselves 50 years into the future and planning our every single action until then to align with that perfectly straight path. Consequently (Conversely?), teenage and "God, I hate the new generation" youth society emphasizes immediate satisfaction, including humongous bangers and risky behaviors. Society constantly praises the superego while denouncing the id, leading to a constant id-loving counterculture in the younger generations. Neither of these paths is the right approach, yet we're stuck in the false hazes of both of them at the same time.

Independence

We should think about both our impulsive desires and our long-term goals. However, our mentalities should not be defined by either, as doing so would create a polarizing, mind-splitting sense of self. We need to focus in on the immediate future, and what we are gonna do with our lives in the days and weeks leading up to the next few years. We don't have to stick straight to the path, we can let loose sometimes and pursue other desires, as long as we are genuine and mindful of what we are pursuing.

I grew up wanting to be a doctor, but music was my drug. If I ever wanted to hide away from my "path towards a doctor," I would play music, I would sing, I would write music. I would pretend like I could possibly succeed as a musician, even though in reality I knew it was a tough world out there for artists. Then I would go back to my studies, knowing that I could probably, most certainly, succeed economically as a doctor. I would lie to myself and simply say that I wanted to be a doctor. But life is so much more than black and white. And life is so much more than money or success in the eyes of society. One of the changes I made to my attitude, which I am most proud of, is that I've decided that I finally know what I want in the immediate future. I want to major in biology and minor in music. Who knows where life will take me afterwards? But in the meantime, I know what I want. Whether it be through medicine or music, I want to connect with other humans and make them feel better.

Now, often when I tell people this, they believe that I've "always had this figured out, lucky him" and then they go back to their mindless day-to-day simply waiting for the next Friday night when they seem to be able to rest. The fact is that understanding your own desires is an extremely tough challenge that requires constant and mindful thought; and just because you haven't figured it out doesn't mean you can't start trying today. I remember telling my mom that perhaps I just wanted to major in biology and see where it goes from there. I was afraid to tell anyone that my long-term has faded out of importance in favor of a short-term. But after openly telling myself and others the truth, I felt relieved. I didn't have to wear a mask and pretend that doctor is the only path society and I will accept. I realized before I even get there, I have many years to make the most out of life and discover what is truly for me. I figured out what I wanted.

After I figured out what I wanted, my own sense of identity and values began to develop. I used to respect my parents' choices without scrutiny or question. I still respect their choices; however, I now also sometimes openly disagree. What we all need to learn is that we can be different in our desires and our beliefs while still respecting others, and that disagreement is not an attack on others. My mom told me that I should value love above all else. But as of right now, I value happiness the most. I'm not sure who is right, or if someone can even be "right" in terms of values, but for the moment, I'm just gonna keep writing this book on finding happiness.

Finally, I believe self-awareness requires an understanding of your own morality. Before becoming a professor at the University of Chicago or Harvard University, Lawrence Kohlberg submitted an unpublished dissertation for his Ph.D. He believed that moral development in humans has 3 separate categories: preconventional, conventional, and postconventional, each with two distinct stages.

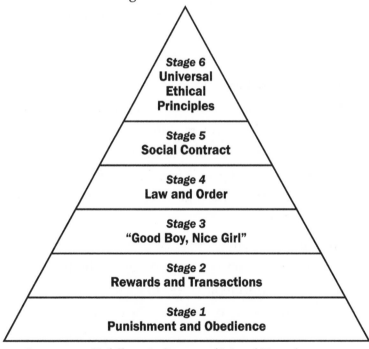

Lawrence Kohlberg's Stages of Moral Development

In preconventional morality, Mr. Preconventional focuses only on himself and believes that intentions do not matter. He doesn't care about doing good, he just does things for himself. In the first stage, Mr. Preconventional solely cares about avoiding punishment. If he can get away with stealing, he will. For example, I may drive above the speed limit if there are no cops around. Except I would NEVER do that... and neither would you, right? In the second stage, Mr. Preconventional begins to care about transactional benefits and rewards. It's similar to saying "what's in it for me?" when your friend asks to copy your homework.

Now, enter Mr. Conventional. He's developed a sense of social norms and the belief that intentions matter. In the third overall stage, he wishes to be a good boy. He's concerned with what others think of him and bases his decisions on what other people think would be the right thing to do. He would get his friend Mr. Birthday Boy a gift for his birthday because others would do the same, and others would think he is a bad friend if he didn't. In the fourth stage, Mr. Conventional becomes obsessed with law and order. Social norms are not the only things that matter... there are literal rules, too. He simply wants to follow the law. Society constructed the rules; therefore they must be valid.

Finally, enter Mr. Postconventional. He has a fully developed, individualized sense of morality. He bases his actions on his own internal moral compass. In the fifth stage, he believes that laws are social agreements that can and should be changed, if need be, for the greater good of humanity. And finally, in the sixth stage, he believes in universal ethical principles. Perhaps one should break the laws if they are unjust.[5]

Each individual decision you make can be based on a different stage of morality—your actions adhere to whichever morality you choose in the moment. Again, I may speed because the cops are not present (stage 1) but then get angry if someone runs a red light (stage 4) while I'm going to a civil disobedience protest (stage 6). Society does not teach us how to postconventionally reason. Rather, society likes to keep us within the conventional orientations because society requires everyone to adhere to a specific set of regulations. I believe that simply staying put inside the conventional can make us mindless servants to society and contribute to the common lack of self-awareness seen today. Often, we do not want to achieve postconventional reasoning because it creates a sense of disagreement that many are not willing to defend; people do not want their beliefs to clash with society's. But I encourage you to discover how your morality may be closer aligned with universal ethical principles than even the law. Martin Luther King Jr. was anything but civil "obedience." Thomas Jefferson, Benjamin Franklin, and John Adams were definitely not thinking about British Colonial Law when drafting the Declaration of Independence. Ultimately, if you understand your own morals, you are more self-aware.

Self-confidence will source us the motivation, and self-awareness will source us the right mindset, to become independent. In healthy independence, we must be able to break free from many dependencies which chain us and realize that "selfishness" is not a bad thing. We should constantly strive for a freedom that provides us an optimal internal state.

I want you to imagine that I am addicted to oatmeal (for those of you who know me, you know for a fact that I am indeed addicted to oatmeal). Specifically, I like low-sugar and high-fiber oatmeal. I eat one bowl every morning, which fills me and provides me the correct nutrients for the day. A low-fat and low-sugar breakfast also helps me make sure I do not eat too much fat throughout the day. But as much as I love oatmeal, I never eat excess. Some days I run out of oatmeal and am disappointed; however, I still eat breakfast.

Now, I want you to imagine that I drink wine with my friends or family every Friday. As much as I love wine (I actually hate wine), I never drink excess. I get tipsy enough to stir a nice, hilarious conversation around me. I don't have a headache the next morning, and I can still remember the conversation pretty well. But I don't simply "get through the week" just to make it to Friday to drink. I can still be open, do goofy things, and rouse hilarious conversation any day that I want.

Unfortunately, the wine scenario above seems almost impossible in America. We are taught by society to become effective workers who have no fun. There is a constant, serious, pretentious aura that covers every open mind. With that comes the "parent demonization of alcohol," with which I'm sure that many are familiar: Your parents partied hard as teenagers and didn't tell their parents. They wanted to escape the pressures of society and showed no moderation in drinking. Enter their teenage kid. They believe that the kid will do the exact same thing, and therefore enact sacred bans and punishments for the child for drinking. However, the scarcity and restrictions that the parents imposed upon alcohol make alcohol seem that much more appealing. You were always denied something that could provide pleasure. Consequently, you party hard as a teenager and don't tell your parents. You want to escape the pressures of society and show no moderation in drinking.

Now, I would like to detail the childhood of my mother. In Beijing, she was given a bowl of alcoholic sticky rice dessert at age 5. She drank it all, fell asleep, and didn't wake up for two days straight. Alcohol was not demonized in Chinese families because parents never got shitface-wasted and therefore neither did the kids. I grew up understanding alcohol and learning how to drink in moderation.

There exists a difference between healthy indulgences and unhealthy dependencies. Healthy indulgences show characteristics of moderation, while unhealthy dependencies often show total submersion and anxious anticipation for the next indulgence. I believe the best way to avoid unhealthy dependencies is to be dedicated towards finding enjoyment in all aspects of life. We should not live to work. Every moment of our lives should count. If we are mindful, we can find things that we truly enjoy and appreciate about our day-to-day. I love sitting in homeroom and talking with one of the coolest teachers ever and three of my fellow swimming teammates. I loved cracking jokes with my biology lab group while we were writing scientific papers. I am grateful that my lab mates were genuinely passionate about learning yet didn't compromise their own enjoyment for the sake of the grade. I think one of the healthiest practices is to think about everything that made you happy at the end of the day. It teaches us soon that happiness can be sent and received anytime, anywhere. We three don't drink or indulge in bad practices because we learned to cherish our day-to-day.

Imagine that I have a girlfriend. I love every moment that I am with her, yet when we are apart, I crave to see her again—nothing else will bring me joy. Again, I would have an unhealthy dependency on my significant other. I've seen many friends have such codependent relationships. We have got to be in control of our own lives and make sure that a new source of happiness is additive to our already abundant lives, not subtractive. We have to be mindful and enjoy every moment and every interaction without getting too needy and greedy for more. We need to be grateful for what we have. Once we create positive energy, more will come to us.

Happiness should be uncompromised in your life. However, we need to dedicate ourselves to getting long-term happiness through meditation and independence. And once you are committed to happiness, happiness is committed to you; and you begin to realize that being "selfish" is not a bad thing. You should treat yourself and ensure that you are doing what is best for you in a way that does not send out negative vibes.

I think a lot of people gave me funny faces when I told them, "I just became a certified cultured pearl specialist with the Cultured Pearl Association of America!" A lot of people questioned why I would ever do that. But the thing is, when it comes to happiness, the only person who has to understand why you do the things that make you happy is you. I love learning, and my certification reflects that.

My at the time best friend once came up to me and was both curious and concerned. A year earlier, I was honored to be invited to perform saxophone in an audition band for the 2018 American Music Abroad Red Tour, touring six countries in central and southern Europe. My friend received the same blessing and was invited to perform with the 2019 Red Tour. However, she seemed notably distracted by something. You see, for years she had spent her summers going to a vacation resort with her close friend — a very nice tradition. She was worried about losing the tradition or angering her friend. She was afraid of losing from something in which she could only win. I promised her that she needed to go out there and do this for herself. A door opened for her to have an amazing time with no regrets. I was excited for her and knew she would grow from the experience. We don't regret the things we have done, we regret the things we didn't do. I hope she could agree with me today that I was determined to convince her to go on the 2019 Red Tour. And in the end, I was so happy to see her photos from Austria.

I also would like to emphasize fighting for what you want and what you believe in. I really dislike conflict; however, I believe it is our duty to ourselves to constantly defend and protect our own principles. If you have watched *The Office*, you know about Toby Flenderson. He is the HR representative for Dunder Mifflin. Michael Scott, boss and protagonist, absolutely hates Toby's guts. He will consistently make fun of, berate, ignore, and throw things at Toby.[6] Toby is genuinely a kind and caring person; however, he quickly backs down and gives up from defending himself or others around him. Obviously, he is a TV character that is meant to portray the extremes of pushoverness in society; however, many people in society still either fight in non-effective ways or do not fight at all. Even when options seem limited, we can always find effective ways.

I have a habit of walking into my AP Psychology teacher's room. Sometimes he's busy helping other students so he kicks me out, but most of the time he lets me stay. In free time, we talk about everything, from Chinese restaurants, to custom-made home countertops, to cottage cheese and grapes (thank you for the suggestion, by the way). He considers himself "the tenth nicest teacher in Bethlehem." But in many ways, I think he is the nicest.

Mr. Ferguson inspires me greatly. He is relaxed, hilarious, and goes with the flow, but not without his own two cents. He has a strong understanding of others and the world around him. He never holds grudges and has always looked at the present and towards the future. He was my teacher at a time that I needed to learn what it meant to be human. And Mr. Ferguson was real. He would get angry at me if I were distracted, but he would also listen to me when I was down. Mr. Ferguson reasonably communicated his frustration with me when I was distracted looking at American art during class. He spent a generous amount of time with me when I was convinced that I was going to die.

When he shows me his values, I want to respect them. And he always respects mine. I walked in one day and was obviously frustrated (and probably overreacting) about something small that happened. You see, before our homecoming football game and homecoming dance, we celebrate a "Spirit Week" at our high school. Each day has a theme to which we dress accordingly. Previous years' Spirit Week days have included Hawaiian shirt day and America day. But this year, we the people were allowed to suggest what themes we wanted for Spirit Week. I heavily advocated for cowboy/cowgirl day, but to no avail. It was the most popular on social media, yes, but it never made it into the Spirit Week list. And additionally, Hawaiian shirt day was removed and replaced with mismatch day. I was infuriated. Hawaiian day and cowboy day were my two high hopes.

Mr. Ferguson understood I was frustrated that I tried lobbying directly with the senior council. So, he suggested something. On mismatch day, I could easily wear Hawaiian shirts and cowboy boots. Additionally, and most importantly, I could convince others to do the same. While direct advocacy did not work, I could inspire a soft "revolution." Psst, spread the word. Underground Hawaiian Cowboy Day.

You can always achieve independence. Although diplomacy didn't work in this scenario, working with others is often the best way. And besides, nobody is forcing me to wear any specific outfit. We can make peaceful statements about what we believe in—cowboy boots and Hawaiian shirts.

Independence

Another important key to independence is realizing that you can't always be there for everyone. Additionally, others should not always be there for you. You need to make your decisions and life choices for yourself and others need to make their decisions and life choices for themselves. One of the most altruistic quotes that I respect, but also with which I disagree completely, comes from the 2006 animated kid's movie *Barnyard*. Ben the Cow says, "Otis, a strong man stands up for himself, a stronger man stands up for others."[7] However, the problem is that we try to bypass standing up for ourselves in order to help others. Before we listen to Ben the Cow, we have to listen to Algernon Sidney. Algernon Sidney, an English politician, opposed divine right of kings, advocated for limited government, and consequently lost his head in 1683 after publishing *Discourses Concerning Government*. Within the text, he states that "God helps those who help themselves."[8] This idea would become greatly popularized in the American colonies with Benjamin Franklin's 1736 *Poor Richard's Almanack;*[9] and I believe anyone and everyone should believe that they can and should help themselves.

My final important aspect of independence is the idea of free will. You may not agree with my perspective on free will; however, I hope we can all share an optimistic idea of how the world works around us. I am a scientist. I believe in the study of the natural world around us. However, I am also a spiritual person. I believe in a total respect and higher explanation of our universe. The debate between fate versus free will is one of the most prevalent questions of mankind. The universe above bestows the gift of life, a highly improbable biological incidence throughout the quiet stars. While it provides and smelts the ore of destiny, it is humans who mold it. I do not believe that everything happens for a specific, methodical reason. Rather, I believe that we can always learn from what happens around us and that we have the power to lead ourselves to our own destiny. We can and should always choose to fight for independence and happiness.

In what seems to be a paradoxical relationship, I am a strong believer in both random variation and meaningful coincidence. I used to tell my friends that when we thought the same thoughts or said the same things, it meant that we were in synchronicity with the universe. Our creation from seed and egg, our genetic makeup, is complete random variation. Yet, the love or connection that two people begin to feel for one another, without having said a word to each other, cannot be explained by the roll of unseen dice. Yes, stumbling upon an old friend at the airport or liking the same music as the stranger next to you is often random, but random can be meaningful if we make it so.

CHAPTER 5

Teenage Relationships

W HEN I WAS IN MIDDLE SCHOOL, I wanted to be a psychiatrist. I wanted to help those around me open up and hopefully change their thoughts from fear to comfort and show them that we have a right to pursue happiness. I wanted to contribute to something greater and prove to them that life is beautiful. I just wanted to care for people. However, in eighth grade, I realized that I could not be a psychiatrist.

I envisioned myself listening to other peoples' stories. Patients told me their traumas, their pains from the past, and all I could do was sit there and listen. Their stories would make me sad, make me angry, make me frustrated at why the world would ever hex another's life with a burden undeserving. Then, I would drive home from work, still thinking about the terrors that indeed exist. I would sit down at the dinner table, still thinking about the world's troubles. I would be torn apart. I had to realize that I was not yet strong enough or capable enough to not only take care of myself, but also take care of others. If I ever wanted to be a psychiatrist, I would have to love myself and unconditionally provide love and support to my patients. I would have to understand that the past cannot be changed. I would have to be able to help others grow while ensuring I was still growing myself.

The mind is a palace of infinite potential that blooms with the bearer. The biggest aspect of teenage relationships is understanding that mentally, most of us have not yet fully bloomed or have even come close to such a thing. Dealing with our own problems is already difficult enough, let alone dealing with others'. Therefore, teenage society is one that can be both pure at its best and gruelingly toxic at its worst, simply because it is hard for us to understand others when we do not even understand ourselves. Nobody is at fault, rather, we need to ensure that we are mindful of ourselves and how we interact with others.

The biggest lesson in relationships came to me from growing distant from my best friend of eight years. He is one of the smartest, strongest, most hardworking, and hilarious people that I've ever met. For years our friend group of five would always hang out together and tell each other everything. We even made a contract, the Brogreement of Bros, which could forever be used to prove that we were a solid bunch who were dedicated to each other.

However, things do not always last. Circumstances change, and so do people and their actions. One friend moved back to England. Our friend group turned from a big circle into a smaller circle and a singular dot, but we still tried our best to keep in touch. And in our sophomore year, the rest of us did not share as many classes together. We soon realized that our friend group had turned from a circle into a square, where each friend was closest to two others but distant from the person "on the opposite corner." Nonetheless, I was still close to my best friend.

We had endless inside jokes and backstories that we intuitively knew about each other. He and I would work together on many projects and assignments while still laughing and making sure we were happy at the same time. Our birthdays are five days apart, and at exactly 12:00AM on each birthday we would send each other huge birthday messages with elaborate stories and punchlines and hidden messages. We would have hilarious banter and deep conversations every week. However, I soon started to have problems with him. I would like to emphasize that *I* started having problems, because things only become problems if you make them problems. He had no problems with me, I was the problematic one.

You see, he was changing as a person. He began to branch out and meet a ton of new people and create a bunch of new friend groups. I was happy for him, but I sometimes wanted to be with him and meet these new people, too. However, he didn't want all of his friend groups to mix. Looking back on it now, that is totally reasonable. Everyone should be allowed to have their own friends untampered by others. But I began to feel unimportant to him. He would sometimes make plans with others and cancel on me, without obvious considerations of me. But I realize now that he didn't cancel on me because he hated me, but rather because he trusted me to be tolerant.

However, I felt differently at the time. I felt neglected and rejected. He went on a trip to Florida with another friend of our group, and neither of them bothered to even let the two of us remaining in New York know. In retrospect they did this to make sure that we were not offended, but we ended up being offended because we discovered by other means. This is when I made it a problem and confronted my best friend. He was very reasonable and promised change and clarity like we used to possess.

In the future, I would tell him when I had a problem, not because I wanted to attack him but rather because I wanted to be completely open with him. But again, my problems are my problems, and not his; and complaints, no matter the intention, are often perceived as hostile. He obviously became frustrated with the fact that I was complaining all the time but didn't show it to me. I believe he did show it to others, though, for example, in his other friend groups. I met one of his new friends at a local festival, but afterwards he complained to others that I was being cocky about meeting new people. Anyway, that lady who I befriended at the festival did not invite me to her bonfire, but rather invited the two from our group who had went together earlier to Florida. She didn't want discord at her bonfire, so I was a potential liability. While there, they played a game of truth or dare. My best friend was dared by my other friend to text me all of his complaints that he voiced about me that night, and not tell me that it was a prank or a joke until three days later:

Juneau, I'm guessing you're angry about us hanging out and not inviting you but that's just how it be. Instead of waiting for you to go off on me though, I'll just send you something. You do things that bother me very often... couldn't you just realize that maybe you could just think about what I want and offer a fair way to compromise? Obviously you are not nearly as self-centered as others but you seem to a lot of the time just think about yourself... Please don't argue back or try to justify yourself because actions speak louder than words.

He knew that I value honesty, clarity, and trust over all other things. I felt terrible, not understanding that that was a "joke" until three days after. I had three days to think about this all to myself. I think that this was the night that changed the course of my life. I finally realized, prank texted or not, that he was genuinely frustrated at me. And I realized that I was unreasonably frustrated at him. Most importantly, I realized that he is his own person. As much as he and I were alike, we were different. And I was unhealthily dependent on him. I expected us to do everything for each other and should've paid more attention to doing things for myself, first.

I hope you understand how I felt excluded, demoralized, and betrayed. However, I also hope you understand that I forgive my friends and understand them better now. Through a bonfire prank, I realized that we need to set the right expectations of ourselves and others so that we protect ourselves and never feel subjugated by another. If we have the wrong expectations, whether it be too selfish, or too selfless, or too demanding, then the people around us will always "disappoint" us. But it's not their fault, it's ours. First Lady Eleanor Roosevelt said it well:

I think [a 'snub'] is the effort of a person who feels superior to make someone else feel inferior. First, though, you have to find someone who can be made to feel inferior.[1]

And eventually, these words would streamline into a powerful quote: "No one can make you feel inferior without your consent."[2] It was extremely important that this happened to me. Was it meant to be? Who knows! But I realized I needed to take care of myself and become independent.

I went out and learned to become independent. I went to Europe and toured with a band. During this time, I ceased most communications back home other than calling my mother and texting my close friend, who would soon become my new best friend. She was kind, caring, and was an outsider with a clearer perspective on the situation than anyone inside. That was when I realized something important: *The people inside the painting cannot see the bigger picture.* I needed to step back with her and understand everything that happened from a generic, yet loving, standpoint. I needed to avoid jumping into situations blindly. I believe talking with her helped me learn how to forgive.

While I was away, the lady who hosted the bonfire and my friend who dared my best friend to send the text message both contacted me. Neither of them was really apologetic, and besides, I didn't expect them to be. They had no reason to be sorry. Rather, they both thought that my purposeful disconnect from my previous best friend and the old social circles was dramatic or immature. That slightly bothered me. They wanted things to go back to the way they were and thought I was without my senses. That's when I had another realization. I had tried to control my former best friend, which is why he was frustrated. Now they were trying to control me, which is why I was currently frustrated. I realized that nobody should try to control anyone. I stood my ground; and fortunately, they soon understood that I just needed time alone.

I forgive them all and am still friends with them today. I think this whole teenage drama chaos was necessary for my growth. While I was away, I also began to realize that *there is a difference between being lonely and being alone.* That forever changed my mindset on relationships and independence.

We should regard each friend at an adequate distance where we give and take only positive energy. Close friends may be close, but they should not be draining of you or require you to sacrifice a part of yourself. Rather, friends must constantly be positive with one another. Such does not mean neglecting bad things or never having negative emotions… it means being open to a full range of emotions, valuing positive energies, and not letting negative emotions soil the good ones.

The hardest part about being a teenager is navigating social approval when you are still trying to find yourself. From a social perspective, almost all adults are uncomfortable around teenagers. In addition, children are sometimes intimidated by teenagers. Teenagers, generation after generation, will always represent the most resented or despised age group. Babies are cute. Elderly people are wise. Adults are hardworking members of society. But we teenagers... we are all reckless, impulsive, spoiled, counterculture-loving fanatics! So, we naturally try to find social approval from our own. However, social approval in teens turns sour pretty quickly.

First, rumors. I want to make this as simple as possible. Don't listen, don't tell. If you promised to keep a secret, keep it. Conversely, if you would like to tell people something personal or a secret, you have to truly trust that the recipient is genuinely a good person. However, I believe that "like attracts like"—if you want to be surrounded by good people, you have to work towards being a good person yourself. Gossip girls attract gossip girls because they share gossip.

I once heard a rumor about me that I would ask this other girl out to prom. I did not let that rumor change my thoughts or actions. I asked someone else who I wanted to ask, and I had a great night. I once heard a rumor about me that I owned a Chinese restaurant and wrote my own little personal love notes inside fortune cookies that I would give this girl who had a boyfriend. It was this rumor that helped me realize that people will believe whatever they want to believe, and that they won't believe the truth if it is more boring than a rumor. And most importantly, I don't have to give a shit about what others think of me.

Secondly, peer pressure. Don't give in. Why should anyone other than you have a say in what you want? However, combating peer pressure is easier said than done.

In fact, giving in to peer pressure originally posed an evolutionary advantage: a great concern for appealing to the nomadic group with whom you hunted and gathered made you less likely to be outcasted or left behind to die. So, we should not beat ourselves up for having socially conformed. Nonetheless, we should stay wary of when and how it occurs, such as with groupthink. Groupthink is when group dynamics and the shared desire for unanimity affect group decision making. Individual members are afraid of expressing doubt or disagreement in fear of social rejection. In addition, being in a group makes individuals feel as if they hold less responsibility. You often get a "unanimous decision" from groupthink that is uncreative and more extreme than any person would individually agree to, such as with the failed Bay of Pigs invasion, as depicted below.

President John F. Kennedy wanted to overthrow Fidel Castro, leader of the new Communist Cuba. He directly inserted himself into the decision making of his subordinates, causing his strategists to develop plans that pleased him rather than plans that were actually strategic.[3] The immediate consequence is known as the Cuban Missile Crisis, where Cuba further backed away from the U.S. in favor of the U.S.S.R. and began building nuclear missile launch sites.

Finally, mob mentality and the toxicity of cliques. Being in a group causes high arousal and low accountability, so people do dumb and mean shit in groups. While sometimes the small societies of each group benefit us in ways that the general society may not (such as a close-knit community of cooperative friends), we need to ensure that we are not fully dependent on the group for our happiness. We need to hold others at a healthy distance so that toxicity does not run deep in the water.

I asked my friend what she thought about her closest group of girlfriends. She responded that they sometimes made her happy and they sometimes made her sad. You see, her friends would constantly bully her and call her nicknames such as "brick," which more girls started to do as well. She never complained, and I could see she was a kind person underneath. She also sometimes had amazing experiences with her friend group. And she smiled and laughed and confided in each of the girls when it was just her and only one of them. She ignored the bad parts and tried to find the good in people. Her tolerance is something I admire to this day, however I wanted her to protect herself. I told her to seriously confront them about how she feels. She agreed with me but was afraid of potentially losing such a big aspect of her life. But even if she felt stuck in the moment, I assured her that branching out in the meantime couldn't be a bad thing. Ultimately, we should never be afraid of protecting ourselves. I hope she can agree with me today.

Now, let us talk about love. Love is a wholesome emotion with many components and aspects. Yale

University professor Robert Sternberg sought to identify what exactly constitutes love and how those factors relate. Throughout his research, he developed the triangular theory of love. He believed three factors interplay to create love—intimacy, passion, and commitment. Intimacy is the closeness and emotional ties that you share with another. Passion is the feeling of emotional stimulation and sexual arousal. Commitment is the conscious decision to continue to stay with another person.[4]

Different combinations of these aspects lead to different types of love. Love with only passion is infatuation, which is evident in the "puppy love" that occurs before a relationship becomes serious. If the relationship grows to include an intimacy component, then it becomes romantic love. If the relationship grows to include a commitment component instead, then it becomes fatuous love. Empty love is when there exists only commitment—no intimacy or passion. This is often found in arranged marriages but can easily blossom to include intimacy and/or passion. If a relationship contains both commitment and intimacy, then it is a companionate relationship. This is what very close friends and family feel between each other.

I believe I had a profound companionate relationship with my close lady friend that I mentioned earlier. She always was so kind and caring to me. When I fell out with my former best friend, she was there to help me through it. When she was having problems with her friend group, I tried my best to be there for her. Her clique of friends would often make fun of her or bully her for being friends with me, in the immature way like "ooo look at that bruise you got! Juneau must have given you a hickey!" or some other silly stuff like that. I only heard about this because my other, trustworthy friends told me. And my friends in the beginning weren't that much kinder with their jokes either. People tried to ruin our friendship, but we didn't give a shit. We talked many nights, and no matter what others said or did, we treated each other well.

Ultimately, when it comes to a significant other, the goal is to achieve consummate love. Consummate love is when intimacy, passion, and commitment are all deeply present. This "perfect couple" would have amazing physical connection for many years, could not imagine themselves happier with anyone else, and would overcome difficulties easily and with grace when with each other.[5]

But in the end, we need to be open and receptive to all kinds of love. I understand it's easy to scoff at parents or be embarrassed by caring, super outgoing friends, but we should always be open and proud to love others. People who think it's "cool" to not say "I love you" back to their kind and caring mothers are really silly. Embrace and give as much love as you can in this world. Love will help you understand your purpose and lead you down the path of happiness in its richest form.

Another thing that teenagers should realize is that we can and should totally feel free to love and date whomever we want. Our significant others in high school most likely aren't going to be who we end up marrying (unless it's the right person), and we need to learn what love is before we find the right people. Also, despite many teenagers' perspectives, going on one date with someone doesn't mean that person is immediately your boyfriend or girlfriend. You do not have to jump so quickly into commitment. You can test the waters first at any time.

The biggest thing you learn from forming relationships in high school with others is that others are different in almost every aspect. They have their own perspectives, ideas, and lives. Some seem to take promises too lightly. Some seem to take promises too seriously. Some seem to stick to methodically-planned hangouts. Some seem to let it slide. I had a friend who changed the date of a hangout 5 times before we got together. I had a friend who I asked to hang out the day of and she committed to it. No matter the case, we have to recognize that we are all just teenagers, and we're still figuring out our values and how we want to act. I have had many times where other people promised to do something with me one day or another just to surmount to nothing. But being angry about how others are will not get me anywhere. Everyone treats promises differently, and some people say promises out of kindness and desire to please while others say promises out of sincerity. I prefer, and believe we should all prefer, sincerity; however, we are all different and we have to respect that.

The next debate that arises is the debate between truth and kindness. When we talk to people, should we prioritize actuality or emotion? There seems to be a gray area in which people should operate. However, we also need to understand what each person prefers. Some people are not yet ready to deal with the truth. No matter the recipient, we should always talk with kindness in mind, and tell the truth in a way that would benefit the person. Telling what I call "positive truth" requires a separation from personal negative biases and a constant search for something positive that you genuinely believe. I don't have to think that a dress is the best dress in existence to tell openly the person that I love the way that the color matches their eyes. And even though some people may be competing with me at saxophone or swimming, I don't have to let that muddy the fact that I genuinely liked their performances.

I think we all need to be more open and compliment others. Yet for some reason, even when we like something about someone, most teenagers seem to not even say a word, especially with men. That frustrates me a ton. What I've noticed with "girl teenage society" is that compliments are given between each other at such a high frequency and with questioning levels of sincerity that girls become completely desensitized to compliments. And conversely, in "boy teenage society," compliments are few and far between, leading to a lack of social love. I believe that this socially-induced deprivation is what causes a guy to think that a girl automatically likes him if she gives him a compliment. Consequently, girls cease to give compliments to guys, because teenage boys and girls would think that the girl likes the guy. Maybe she does, but we don't have to be immature assholes about it. I think we should all just give genuine compliments to everyone.

Okay, now that I've started complaining about teenage trends, I'm gonna keep going. Passive aggressive communication is not something that you should ever do to a friend or significant other. I know many people do not do this, but I want to get this straight: it is stupid to deal with problems by saying "I'm fine" or "it's whatever" to something that totally is not fine. In addition, compliment fishing is terrible. In my opinion, saying "I'm so ugly" to get someone to call you pretty only brings more negative energy to you, and creates an unhealthy dependency of backwards and self-deprecating validation. Reverse psychology to get someone to comfort you is playing an emotional game of tug of war. If you want comfort, you can ask for it. If you need help, you can ask for it. Do not automatically assume that people will help you if you say "it's fine." Being direct and honest in a constructive way will help create positive energy. Thank you for listening to my rant.

We also have to be constructive when we deal with other people. Simply put, we should never burn bridges or close doors. Destruction is one of the worst things someone could do, yet people do it often. They will badmouth ex-friends or try to hurt people. I was threatened and almost physically attacked by a third person after a friend and I had a mutual falling out. That was when I realized that some people do not want to build the tall LEGO skyscrapers that I want to. Some people want to watch the world burn if it does not align with their wants. We need to forgive those around us and leave still-standing things as they were. If we constantly stoop to the level of lowness, we will encourage a regressive society. If we constantly take the high road, we will help advocate for a progressive society.

I like to tell those around me "healthy thoughts and healthy words." I believe we can and should fight for what we want, but we have to pick our battles wisely. We should make each mission with little resistance both internally and externally. The first step is believing in your own intentions. The second step is realizing that other people may not believe your intentions and will rather assume them from what you say. Therefore, we need to speak with "positive truth" and with fact. The words we say either need to be cautionary or healthy, or else we risk immediately offending or scaring someone. Here is an iMessage that a very close friend of mine sent me:

FRIEND. This guy said the weirdest shit today. I need

to tell someone!!! It was sooo awkward. There was a school shooter on his campus and he texted me and was like… "I might die today, and unfortunately we're still not together in the end." And I was like uhhhhh awkward.

JUNEAU. What the f*ck… I don't think this is an appropriate time to say 'uhhhh awkward'… It was a school shooter! It isn't kind of you to say that after someone opens up because they're afraid of dying!

FRIEND. First off… he was joking…

If you were shocked by the first text… yeah, I was, too. The delivery of what you say is RIDICULOUSLY IMPORTANT and needs to be thought out before you cause people to freak out or have a heart attack. Don't worry, I am especially pissed that the guy joked about there being a school shooter. However, I hope you understand why I was angry for a split second at my close friend. I know this is an extreme example, but delivery comes in a million ways that can do good or harm. We need to at least seem optimistic or positive in our speech, because spreading negative energy will cause a lot of problems.

There was one time that I was very angry. A bunch of my friends, including me and my best friend, made a dumb mistake. My best friend and I had to cover for my other friends. I was so pissed nobody else was willing to admit the truth, so I told my best friend "I hate defending these cowards." I thought nothing of it at the moment, but he later accidentally said in an outrage "why am I defending cowards?" right in front of the other friends. That was when I realized mental thoughts and word choice both need to be thoroughly processed in the mind to make sure that we only spread positive, or factual, energy.

A good way to go about talking about things to others in a healthy manner is something we learn in elementary and middle school and forget for the rest of our lives. It's called the "I" voice. When in conflict, we need to start every sentence with "I." If you are bothered because someone seems to ignore you, you do NOT say "you don't care about anyone." Accusative language immediately causes the recipient to go into defense mode and refuse to acknowledge, let alone understand, your perspective. A better way to go about this would be to say, "I feel as if you sometimes do not value what I have to say." I understand how tempting it is to say, "you absolute bitch" or "f*ck you," but that will more often than not just worsen the situation for you both. People will not even think about changing for better if you just tell them to screw themselves.

One of the beliefs that best keeps me away from destructive tendencies is that of karma. What goes around, comes around. If I put out positive energy by forgiving, then positive energy will find its way back to me. And if someone else brings negative energy to the table, I do not have to occupy myself with "punishing them" or "teaching them a lesson," because, in all reality, I trust that the universe itself will do that, heheh.

The hardest part about writing about teenage relationships is the fact that I have to write about teenage relationships. The actions of teenagers, for lack of a better word, can be "cringey." We have the tools to create and destroy but have not yet fully grown into understanding how to use them. However, it is important that we make mistakes and learn from them. I would not be where I am today if none of the above scenarios ever occurred. To hide our past is to pretend that they never existed at all. I want to remember every good and bad thing that has happened to make sure I grow as a person. We need to be committed to staying strong and improving no matter what curveballs life throws at us.

Part of me again dreams of becoming a psychiatrist. I want to help those around me open up and hopefully change their thoughts from fear to comfort and show them that we have a right to pursue happiness. But teenage relationships showed me that nothing is a straight path. Life will ensure we have the craziest journeys; all we can do is open our eyes and try to understand the world around us.

ENTR'ACTE

WHAT DO I LOVE TO DO?
This is a question I am asked a lot on my college applications. What do I love to do? Well, I like music. That's a given. I also like biology. I like writing, swimming, talking, and a bunch of other things. But I sit down at my college application and those activities don't feel like enough. Don't get me wrong, I love music and biology and writing and swimming and talking. But my favorite activities somehow feel like they should be things I do *all* the time.

There are two activities that I do more than anything else—more than swimming, more than doing homework, even more than *eating food*. The two things that I love to do are two of the simplest, yet two of the most important: thinking and remembering.

First, thinking. One of my favorite things to do is to ask a question and figure out the answer myself. My best example of this was when my friends and I were doing breath training for swimming. If you've ever gone from one side of the pool to the other without breathing, you get the sensation that you need to pee. I simply asked them, "Do you guys feel like you need to pee every time we reach the other end of the pool?" To my astonishment, yes. It's not just me (in hindsight, *thank God* it's not just me). Everyone around me also needs to pee.

So, this begs a bigger question. *Why do we all need to pee?* So, I figure out the logic in my head. First, none of us are asking our bodies to pee, so this is definitely instinctive. Nobody here is asking his or her bladder to burst. Secondly, we are going long amounts of time without oxygen. We are without a resource that we need.

I came up with my conclusion. If you held your breath long enough, you would eventually... release both fluid and solid excrement until you either got oxygen or died. The instinctive "I need to pee" is the body trying to release bodily wastes so that they do not toxify the rest of the body in the lack of oxygen. My mind is full of random, burning questions that I seek to answer and explain.

Secondly, remembering. If you ever decide to write a diary, you will one day look back upon your written accounts of past days and realize that some of your experiences are absolutely insane. You will reflect and feel like "there's no way this actually happened." But yeah, it did. And it was funny, too. Anyway, here are some of my craziest experiences throughout the years...

In freshman year, I was elected into the student senate. I had to switch to a new homeroom where all senators met and discussed problems and solutions every morning.

However, there existed a slight intermediate problem. During the time of my switch, the school was also taking yearbook pictures, and yearbook pictures were organized and delivered by homeroom. Most other students had pre-printed and already-distributed yearbook picture forms that they could simply hand to the photographer. Because I was in the process of switching homerooms, I did not have a pre-printed form. I had to work with an older man, seemingly grumpy and reserved, to handwrite me a new form.

First mistake: my name is "Juneau." He looked at me like I'm speaking an alien language. Who the hell is named "Juneau"? Nonetheless, I spelled my name out for him to write down.

But here's the thing. I was watching him write my name, and his handwriting... looked as if he had never written before. It was boxy and angular and there really shouldn't be any boxy or angular letters in my name. Something was off. I thought maybe he didn't hear me. I decided to ask. That was my second mistake.

"Did you get that?"

"Yep."

"You sure?"

He then stared at me with the face of death. The stare of a million dark voids encircling the fragile universe. A long, grumpy, impatient stare. I then decided it was in my best interest to shut up, even though his handwriting itself looked like an alien language. I just hoped that whoever got the form could read it. Spoiler alert: nobody ever did.

Fast forward from October to June. The yearbooks were finally on sale. I felt accomplished after having survived my first year of high school. I pick up my yearbook from the school store and try to find myself and my friends.

But according to the yearbook, "Juneau Wang" didn't exist. No, he never went to high school. He was a phantom of nothing, cursed to forever be hidden from the world of meaning. His achievements and memories were robbed by the face of another man: Gunehu Whng.

Hello, my name is Gunehu. Take me to your leader.

Juneau Wang? He was under the "not pictured" section. He never happened. But Gunehu? Gunehu was a student senator. Gunehu was in the jazz band and on the swimming team. Gunehu also had no vowels in his last name.

I leave this memory with a few conclusions. One, I definitely looked at the face of death. Two, there's no point in denying it: *someone* here is an alien.

But this wouldn't be the last time I felt as if someone were an alien, or as if I were tempting death. In fact, both of those happen again at different times in my swimming career...

I was sitting on the bench, getting ready to swim at the weekend invitational. But I heard my name—I heard people cheering for me. Except it was not directed at me. It felt as if people were screaming "Juneau" to some other person, maybe somebody already in the water. I didn't think much of it. But then some of my teammates walked back to the bench from the racing pool and stared at me with utter confusion:

"Juneau, weren't you just... swimming?"

"What? No, I've been here the whole time."

We then all stared at the cooldown pool, scanning for anything unusual. And there was the man who just swam, who caused all this confusion... me? It looked like me, but with a smaller head and a larger body. He had the same big ears. He had the same goofy smile. He had the same forehead. He even had the same goggles and swimsuit.

They say that there are seven people in the world who look exactly like you. And for some reason, I met my doppelgänger at a swim meet in upstate New York, 30 minutes from my home.

I believed in both random variation and spiritual coincidence. However, at that time I also truly believed in aliens. No, my doppelgänger is not an alien, but how could we only live a few hours away from each other? Aliens, that's why.

The Day That I Lived

I woke up one morning and felt a sharp pain in my chest. It felt like a small arrow underneath my sternum. My coughs were raspy and felt like they were pulling energy away from my soul. I felt a throbbing sensation in my left throat. It was like something was stuck. It was something that I had never felt before. It was not bacteria or a virus or some illness. It was not some muscle soreness or tiredness or pain. It was as if I were completely fine yet also stabbed in the heart. I felt heavy, as if I were sinking into the ground, but also light, as if my weight meant nothing on Earth. I felt strength in my muscles but weakness in my conscience.

I told my mom, and she told me to be careful. She seemed very concerned. She gave me some herbal medicine and said that I could've had some blood circulation problems in the night, perhaps even a clot.

While I was driving to school, I started thinking about what a blood clot could really mean. But thinking about it only made it worse. A blood clot could cut off circulation to important parts of the body. Maybe my heart would fail to beat correctly. Maybe my head would break down. I began thinking about how I could have a stroke. I convinced myself that I either escaped death through the night or was going to die very soon. And to top it all off, I had a swim meet that afternoon, and I was swimming long distance.

God, I thought to myself, if I didn't die last night, I will most certainly die by doing long distance swimming. I was sure that my heart would give out to the stress and somehow, someway, I would collapse and cease to exist.

I went to the nurse's office. Before the nurse herself was available, I just talked to the receptionist. I told her everything. How I felt, both emotionally and physically. I tried masking my internal fears, because I know other people don't need to see that. I showed myself as strong and capable and relaxed. That helped me for a little bit.

I then went into the examination room. My vitals seemed okay, but I still had pain. I couldn't explain it, and neither could she. She told me to check in periodically throughout the day. Wow, that's wonderful, I thought. Nobody knows what's wrong with me, yet I can feel it.

I kept to myself for most of the school day. I decided to just think about everything. I love swimming long distance, but I'd really hate to die. Imagine feeling a haze over you. It's not any color or of any scent, it's just there. You feel as if you're staring at the world and in the corner of your eyes is always something watching you, waiting for your actions. Imagine feeling like you are going to burst, but also collapse, inside.

Did I die? No. I told my coach my heart hurt, and I swam shorter distance events that night. I woke up the next day perfectly fine, and I am blessed for that. I don't know how to explain death to you, and I can't convince you that I was close to death, but for one day I truly believed in it. And that was one of the most important days of my life.

I thought about how fragile we all are. We can be taken away in an instant. I looked over my life. Did I make mistakes? Yes. But I didn't regret them because I learned to learn from them. Did I live each day pursuing happiness? I surely thought so. But I wasn't ready to die. I didn't want to go.

Before, I used to think that I could be okay with death knowing that I lived every day as if it were my last. But on that day, I realized that my commitment fell through—I no longer was living every day as if it were my last. I was taking time for granted.

I wanted life so badly. I just wanted one more night. I promised myself something. God, if I lived to see the end of my swim meet, I would go home, put on some fancy clothes, and ask my friend to get ice cream with me. Then, I would drive her home and ask her out on her driveway.

I lived to see the end of my swim meet. And I stuck to my promise to God. She said no, she wasn't interested. But that's okay. Because in the face of death I did something I never had the confidence to do before. And even though she rejected me, I was satisfied. I knew in my pained heart that at least I committed myself to living that day as if it were my last.

I don't know how to explain death to you, and I can't convince you that I was close to death, but for one day I truly believed in it. And that caused me to go for what I want and live life to the fullest.

Entr'acte

The Day That I Had Too Much Fun

I went out with my friends one night. A fond memory of ours as children was going to the local laser tag arcade. So we went there after many years. We played two games of laser tag. As a kid, I always thought I was good at laser tag, but obviously in hindsight I was definitely not. But I tried my best as a new teenage boy and got onto the leaderboards for my sharpshooting skills. No big deal.

Another thing that happens as a teenager is that you become more impulsive. As kids, we would never take out quarters to gamble on the claw machines with prizes inside or the "spin the wheel" games that give you tickets. However, we teens wanted to beat the system. We felt smarter and had high self-efficacy. We won a few rubber ducks and some candy.

Then I eyed another arcade machine in the corner. I quickly looked into my wallet and found it empty of quarters. I begged my friend for some, promising it would be for good use. I ran over to Guitar Hero Arcade.

I stuffed the machine with quarters and played the only song I recognized: "Rock You Like a Hurricane" by the Scorpions. My friends surrounded me as I mashed the keys on the guitar controller. I sped through the song on hard difficulty.

As a kid, I always wanted to get the high score on one of the arcade games. I wanted the world to see how cool I was. As a teen, I made it a reality. The high score before I finished

"Rock You Like a Hurricane" was around 44,000 points. Let's just say I got 96,000 points.

I was ecstatic. By now it was past the junior license driving curfew of 9:00PM but I didn't care anymore. I was a winner. At around 12:00AM we went out to Denny's and I was in an amazing mood. I had this delicious Grand Slamwich. It had sausage, bacon, ham, scrambled eggs, and American cheese on potato bread, served with hash browns and maple syrup.

The Denny's smelled of weed. Soon, a few police officers pulled in. I was anxious and afraid initially. I didn't want to get caught as a junior driver. But I soon realized they weren't there to check me, obviously. They weren't even there to investigate the heavy fumes of weed. Someone else called the cops because a big group table was giving the waitress a hard time. I'm also pretty sure they attempted to dine and dash.

We left around 1:00AM. At this point, I was driving three of my friends home. Except I accidentally took a wrong turn and ended up on the highway. I realized I would have to pay a toll and was freaking out. I never had paid a toll before. My good friend and I decided that we could both pitch in 30 dollars and hopefully that would be enough for the toll.

But it gets worse. Driving up to the toll booth, there was a cop, who seemed like he was inspecting each car and driver that passed through the gate. Now I was afraid.

There was almost a 100% chance he would look at us teens and look at my junior license and realize that (1) it is slightly past 9:00PM and (2) there are more than 2 people in this car.

I was shaking. And then something flashed before my eyes. On the opposite side of the gate, a car didn't want to pay the toll and sped through the gate, almost running over the cop. He stumbled and stood up in shock and quickly got in his cruiser and chased down that car.

I got up to the gate and smiled at the lady manning the toll booth. I asked her how much it would be.

"That'll be 30 cents."

For many reasons that night, I had too much fun. And considering not only the law but also my general health and safety, it was definitely a risky night. I won't ever do that again. But in the end, I'm glad I'm still alive, and I'm sure as hell proud that I have the highest score for Guitar Hero.

Mornings

6:20AM. The alarm shouts at me, jolting me from calm existence to immediate anger and frustration. I get up, quickly get changed, and go downstairs. Usually my mother is awake at this time, but the house is quiet and dark.

Seriously? I think to myself. How could my mother forget to wake up? Angrily, I begin to make breakfast and get everyone's stuff ready. I always start with my own bowl of oatmeal. I let the oatmeal sit for a little and quickly print an essay for English class that I forgot to print the night before. Except the paper tray is empty. Of course, on the one day that I have to make breakfast, I also have to take a new ream and refill the printer. I cuss to myself.

It is only when I sit down that I check my phone. I begin to eat my oatmeal. None of my friends are responding either. I check my email:

Thursday, Feb. 28: All schools will operate on a two-hour delay today.

I look outside. The entire neighborhood is covered in white snow, shining and glistening as the sun rises.

I stop eating my oatmeal. I go up the stairs back to my room. I put on my pajamas and sleep.

Bao

I don't cry often. But there was one time where the tears ran down my cheeks without any notice. Nothing asked for my permission. Teardrops condensed from a bucket of emotion that filled so quickly. I was in English class, the teacher showing us Pixar short films for fun.

In Toronto, a Chinese-Canadian woman makes a bao breakfast for her husband. She excitedly anticipates their meal together. The ability to enjoy food together is one of the most important values of Chinese culture. But unfortunately, the husband is running late and must quickly stuff his face and leave. The woman sighs and continues to eat. But all of a sudden, one of the steamed buns comes alive.

At first shocked, she soon realizes that the little bao is a baby and must be taken care of. While the husband is at work, she raises the steamed bun. They practice tai qi together in the park and eat pastries together on the bus ride home from the market. But eventually, the bao grows and becomes a teenager and desires independence from the mother. He wants to play soccer with the other teenagers, but the mother is afraid of him getting hurt and drags him away from the soccer field. She wants more attention from him but feels ignored. She offers a pastry on the bus, but this time he does not accept.

The steamed bun grows more and more distant. The mother makes a big dinner for them to share, but he goes out with his cool teenager friends instead. She eats the entire dinner out of frustration and loneliness. And when he comes home, he has an engagement ring and a blonde fiancée. He packs his stuff and tries to walk out the door for good, but the mother stops the bao. In a fit of rage, the mother eats the steamed bun. After realizing what she has done, she cries hard and heavy.

The mother wakes up from her dream, terribly saddened. Her real son enters the room, prompted by father to apologize to her. The son offers the same pastry to the mother as the mother did the bao in the dream. They share the pastry on the bed and cry. In the end, the whole family, including the son's fiancée, make steamed buns together by the table.[1]

Part of me was shocked that I cried in class. Part of me was disgusted that nobody else cried. Without any dialogue, that film plucked chords within my heart. Maybe the people around me would never understand.

No, I'm not sad that the mother ate the bao. No, I'm not sad because they are crying. I'm crying because of the growth of the bao, raised Chinese but also adapting to Western society. I'm crying because of the food uneaten and not enjoyed together. I'm crying because of the empty nest syndrome, something I can't even begin to comprehend myself. The struggle between independence, attention, and love.

In *Bao*, I almost understood the pain and struggles my parents felt. Who am I to them, a reckless teenager? And who were they to their parents? Do all teenagers abstain from their seats at the dining table? It is a newstruck pain I feel but cannot comprehend.

The mother loves the steamed bun. The mother loves the steamed bun with all her heart. But the bao is human, too. He has his own desires and life ahead of him. She cannot keep him forever. She cannot control or keep or forever protect what she holds so dearly. Literature time and time again shows us what happens. And somehow, we all understand the idea of this feeling. We love something so much that we would rather destroy it or capture it ourselves so it never leaves. It is what I call the archetype of primal love, I believe the most intense love out there. If I can't have you, nobody will.

What resonates and ripples within the well of the soul is different between each of us. I hope you see how and why I spontaneously cried. It's not only about the steamed bun. I hope that one day people will understand the literary, social, and psychological magnificence that is *Bao*.

The Day That I Accidentally Bought Alcohol

I had a few minutes of spare time. The sky was a beautiful blue, speckled lightly with fluffy yet fragile clouds. The sea in front of me was a dark blue, ebbing and flowing all around. I jumped into the water. The cool waves surrounded me and tickled my skin. The sea comforted me and hugged me under the warm sun. I was being cared for by the Adriatic Sea.

Behind me was Croatia, and in front of me was the entire Mediterranean. Above me was the sun, and below me was sea urchins.

I stepped on three sea urchins. Their spines got stuck in my feet. Don't worry, the spines would come out... eventually.

Anyway, a few days later I walked into the town of Poreč with my friends. We were taking a daybreak from performing with American Music Abroad. We wandered down the tiled alleys, surrounded with shops on both sides. One advertisement in particular caught my eye—a sign that read "BETTER SEX." I went up to the sign and into the shop. Inside I found a small, glass bottle, filled with water and a leaf. It looked something like tea or an herbal drink. My friends suggested that I gift it to one of the more flamboyant people in the band. Then the shopkeeper came up to me:

"You want?"

"No, no, it's okay."

"But it give you better sex."

I thought about it for a solid 10 seconds and then said yes. I gave her my money and left with a bottle of better sex. My friends and I agreed to each take a swig on the tour bus.

Before leaving town, I made one last stop. My friends wanted to shop, but I was interested in something else. I saw a beautiful arch over one alleyway. It was an entrance, adorned in gold and mosaic. There was a mosaic of Jesus, he who says *ego sum ostium per me si quis introierit salvabitur*—I am the door; by me, if anyone shall enter, he shall find salvation. I know not much about the New Testament, but in hindsight, that was quite an adequate verse to put on an entrance.

I walked into the Euphrasian Basilica. There existed a kind of truth within its walls. Something I had not felt in a long time. Its columns were old, its arches were exposed brick, but I felt that its sentiment and spirit truly transcended the aesthetic. I felt an adrenaline rush in there. I felt alive.

There was a small and antique courtyard. There was a simple room for ceremony. I keenly watched the mosaics. It was perhaps some of the least-realistic religious art I have ever seen, but it meant something to me. I could feel the icons. I don't know if what I felt was God or Jesus, but I felt something.

I returned to the courtyard. I climbed the bell tower. I felt my weight on the thin steps as I ascended up the narrow stairway. And when I reached the top, I could see the world. The beauty that is Croatia. The sky was the same beautiful blue. The water was now clear and light. The pastel orange-colored roofs and tan brick walls dotted the beautiful Earth. The short moment lasted forever. And forever lasted only a second. I walked out of the basilica happy. I walked out of the basilica as my ideal.

On the bus, we showed everyone my purchase. My friend opened the cap, smelled the bottle, and… closed the bottle. She looked at the bottom of the bottle to see if there were any nutritional facts. We didn't know a lick of Croatian, but she recognized a few simple words: "50% BRANDY."

Holy shit, I thought to myself. I accidentally bought alcohol. I was only 16, under the legal age for Croatia and most certainly under the legal age for my American band group. I hid my face under the bus seats and didn't want to look at everyone around me. It was alcohol. I begged them to keep quiet. I was so afraid of getting in trouble. I asked my friends who were with me on the trip to throw it away somewhere for me. I most certainly did not want it back.

My friends disposed of it, and a tremendous weight lifted off of my shoulders. I felt redeemed. I constantly look back on my decisions that day and I respect every single one of them. I was a young and idealistic man. I was enlightened. I broke the law, but I was one with the universe. I'm not sure what this story provides other than a few laughs. But I'm proud of the day that I accidentally bought alcohol.

CHAPTER 6

Adult Relationships

I WOULD LIKE TO DISCUSS teenage relationships with adults by first talking about babies. As most can agree, we were all babies at one time or another. For many reasons, a lot of adults seem to suppress or reject the fact that they were once teenagers when talking with other adults, or with us teenagers. So, let's just focus on babies for a bit.

As we begin to develop, we are simultaneously affected by both nature and nurture. There are things we cannot change as babies, including our inherited characteristics, biological sex, legal dependency status, and tax returns. Well, actually, we cannot change our *family's* tax returns as babies, but we do serve as a tax benefit to our parents. Anyway, we are also greatly affected by the environment around us. And eventually, we realize that we can influence the environment ourselves, and we become the "little scientists" who actively seek understanding of the world around us. Although we do not realize it until much later, our composure can affect the composure of those around us, and vice versa.

First, I would like to discuss the temperament of babies. Psychologists Alexander Thomas and Stella Chess conducted short questionnaires examining infant temperaments for respective parents, and early childhood teachers. They specifically recorded variables such as activity level, regularity, adaptability, distractibility, and approach or withdrawal. From their data, they concluded that around 60% of children fall into one of three categories of temperament: easy, difficult, and slow to warm up.

Easy children were exactly that. They regularly ate, slept, and had a positive attitude or approach when responding to new situations. They smiled, were mostly in a good mood, and could accept frustration with little fuss or outbreak. However, problems most often occurred when the child was placed into situations in which required responses, tasks, or activities of the child were different than those of the home. Imagine if I, a child, grew up at home smiling and knowing that if I said "please" and "thank you," I would be rewarded with a smile back. What happens when I go to a strict daycare center, where the caretakers don't smile back? I become frustrated. What the heck, fake mommy?

Difficult children were the opposite of easy children. They are slow to get used to change and have irregular eating, sleeping, pooping and peeing cycles, characterized by a negative attitude or approach and frequent crying and tantrums. Problems most often occurred during socialization, such as with peer groups, school, and dealing with the expectations of parents and others.

Slow to warm up children were intense and displayed negative responses similar to difficult children when exposed to new scenario, but gradually adapted, like easy children. An in-between category, problems for the children varied between cases.[1]

Secondly, we should discuss attachment styles. Attachment is the emotional bond that forms between the infant and the caregiver. Attachment is gradually developed throughout the first six months of life and then becomes evident in the following six months. Investigating attachment, psychologist Mary Ainsworth conducted an experiment investigating how different children would react to the presence (or lack thereof) of their mothers or a stranger. This is commonly referred to today as the "strange situation" experiment. All kids with their mothers are first introduced into a controlled room with toys. The kids would play with the toys, and the mother would either leave the room or a stranger would enter. The results led Ainsworth to develop three general attachment styles: secure, avoidant, and ambivalent.

Secure infants would explore the room and toys happily and confidently in the presence of their mothers. However, secure infants always made sure to touch base with mommy every once in a while. They were wary around strangers, but calm if mom were near. If mom left, they would be obviously upset. It was found that mothers of secure infants were loving, warm, responsive, and greatly sensitive to the infant's needs, leading to a nice, perfect mutual relationship. In my own opinion, this is an example of consistent and clear communication.

Avoidant infants did not touch base nor look at the stranger nor mother. They seemed nonchalant and ambivalent, showing no interest or concern in exploring and little reaction to the presence or absence of the mother or stranger. Imagine if you had a child who didn't care you existed! Mothers of avoidant infants seemed unresponsive, insensitive, and coldly rejecting. Ainsworth in her narrative theorized that avoidant infants avoided their mothers when they had a history of rejection or erratic attachment development. The child, perhaps, learns due to the actions of the caregiver that the communication of needs has no influence on the caregiver or the situation.

Ambivalent infants had mixed feelings. They were clingy and unwilling to explore. They were generally upset by the stranger, regardless of the presence of the mother. They were hard to sooth and often showed mixed and ambiguous reactions, as if tasks attempted by the caregiver constantly, and successfully, failed. Imagine, for example, trying to talk to a baby. You have absolutely no idea what the hell it wants, but it keeps crying and shaking and peeing. You feel you can't do anything and wish the baby could just fricking speak. As expected, mothers constantly tried pleasing the infant but were inconsistent and insensitive.[2] We are a long way away from understanding how babies work, but the main theory behind the development of ambivalent attachment is that it is a "strategy"—a response to unpredictable caregiving—to show baby face helplessness or anger, which could help keep the caregiver paying attention and help the baby maintain control of the interaction.[3] When I think of it this way, it almost makes sense. Like, I'm pretty sure we've all seen some teenagers and adults try to get attention this way. I personally theorize that insecure attachment styles can and will continue throughout development if the child cannot find a source of consistent security.

There is a fourth attachment style that is puzzling and highly debated, but necessary to discuss. Graduate student of Ainsworth, Mary Main added the "disorganized/disoriented" attachment. If the infant does not seem to even consistently try to achieve even relative proximity with the caregiver, it is known as "disorganized." These infants are characterized with displays of fear, freezing, dissociation, and jerky movements. The infants would have eyes turned away from the mother and seemed dazed and depressed.[4] Mary Main later found that most mothers of disorganized/disoriented children had suffered major losses or trauma and became severely depressed around the time of the birth of the infant. They even found that around 56% of mothers who had lost a parent before they completed high school then had children with disorganized/disoriented attachments.[5]

The interaction between babies and parents is extremely complex. Similar to reciprocal determinism, factors are constantly affecting each other. Imagine if you had a difficult and avoidant baby. Or, conversely, imagine that you had a parent who were unreliable and insensitive. I'm not sure which comes first, but I am certain that difficult parents and difficult babies develop together. However, parents constantly have the choice to not be difficult.

I am blessed to have had kind and loving parents. They were not perfect, but they knew that I trusted that they were doing what was best for me and helped me become who I am today. However, I have met some adults who are total and complete assholes. I see it in the way they talk to others. I see it in the way they talk to their kids. Adults wonder why teenage rebellion occurs. But it isn't as simple as blaming bad parents.

The foundations of our lives come from what our parents give us. The foundations of their lives come from what their parents gave them. If parents had bad parents themselves, then we are stuck in a never-ending loop of troubled parents and troubled kids. The hardest path that a parent can and should take is breaking the cycle for the better. But it's easier said than done.

I view parents similar to the way I view government. Note that I said government, not politics. The relationship between a child and a parent should be a mutual contract in the name of love and in the building of trust where the parent uses his or her control to promote the healthy and best interests for the child and the child in turn respects the parents for such and is allowed to execute control of his or her own life. But what are "healthy" or "best" interests?

I want to first discuss the authoritarian parent. Mr. Authoritarian is stern, rigid, and overly concerned with the rules. He dictates that there exist no exceptions to the rules, not even for his own child. His child, Mr. Authoritarian Jr., then grows up and becomes a conventional member of society. Mr. Authoritarian Jr. most certainly can become successful. However, Mr. Authoritarian Jr. is mindless, has never experienced being allowed to control his own life, and will not question the rules of society. He will cave into social norms and will not obtain or understand universal ethical principles or even genuine love. He may become insecure, timid, withdrawn, negative, or self-destructive. He will understand only conformity and deprivation of the id.

Except, I lied. There's another option for that child. He may not grow up to be Mr. Authoritarian Jr., he may grow up to be Mr. Rebellious. Mr. Rebellious will spite his parents for years to come. Mr. Rebellious will also see no value in rules and consequently make many poor choices that may endanger his health and the health of those around him. Even if Mr. Authoritarian truly loved his child, he did not promote the best interests.

Teenagers need their parents to not be too strict to the detriment of growth. When parents sometimes bend the rules for their child, the child feels a sense of love, understands that intimate connection has benefits, and is allowed to realize that laws, or other people, may not always be "right" according to universal ethical principles. This creates loving, self-confident pioneers of society who concern more for the current welfare of the people than the pieces of paper written by the dead. And when parents give freedom and allow teenagers to make their own choices, such as allowing them to go to their friends' house and sleep over one free night, or allowing them to eat what they want, or not cramming their schedules with too much family time or other activities dictated by parents, teenagers will be more likely to respect and admire their parents.

Now, we are going to talk about the punishing parent. Mrs. Punishment constantly uses punishment to weaken what she considers "bad behavior" of her kid. She takes away her kid's phone. She spanks her kid. But the thing is, simply punishing a kid for doing something wrong does not provide any guide to what is the correct or model behavior. Constant punishment, especially physical, can cause avoidance, lying, anxiety, fear, and aggression in the child. If you constantly use punishment, then you are promoting the values of a regressive society. If you use physical punishment, you are proving to your child that violence is the answer. Kindness and love are extinguished. These children will often become bullies of their own because they desire, just like Mrs. Punishment promoted, to have control by fear. They will fail to understand true forgiveness, tolerance, or acceptance.

Let me put it this way, if my momma raised me right (and I know she did), and I made a small mistake, I would feel bad about making that mistake. If I told her about it, and she scolded me but also forgave me, I would still feel bad about the mistake, but would be relieved that someone could still accept me for not being perfect. I would end up learning honesty, acceptance, and love. If she immediately took my phone away, I would never again open up to her. Parents are not the justice system; parents are supposed to show you that love and kindness mean more. It's simple economics: if you want your kid to do something, you need to have both accurate incentives and accurate policy.

Before I introduce the next parent, I would like to talk about an extremely common dynamic between teenagers and parents. I like to call it the love/independence balance. Most parents love their children. But most children also want independence. Parents need to ensure that their desire for love does not turn into vicarious control of their children's' lives. I have friends who, although fully licensed, have their parents drive them to many places. Their parents are supportive, driving their kids to all swim meets, all music performances, and school. Obviously, circumstances and the desire to support your child come into play. But we all need to realize that teenagers are gonna grow up and will have to learn how to do things themselves. Some of the best lessons I have ever learned were while driving myself to my own auditions and exams, cooking my own food, crashing my own bike, and managing my own schoolwork without parents harping me (or actually, even knowing) about my grades. It allowed me to better respect what parents do for their children and respect the lives of others in general. A healthy amount of independence made me love them even more, because they raised me to be my own man. Parents—your kids are not gonna be dependents forever, so stop forcing them to be ones.

Okay, now enter Mr. Permissive Neglectful. For example, Mr. Dursley from *Harry Potter and the Sorcerer's Stone* has traits of both authoritarian and permissive neglectful. He is demanding and he doesn't give two shits about Harry. He is cold, unloving, and indifferent, forcing Harry, who he grudgingly took in after the death of Harry's parents, to live in a cupboard under the stairs.

And with him, enter Mrs. Permissive Indulgent. Mrs. Dursley loves to indulge her son Dudley and cares even less for Harry. She is way too involved and loves her little angel

Dudley no matter what. Even if Harry is right and Dudley is wrong, Dudley will still get the delicious food and love and Harry will get constant rejection.[6] Harry is a good example of a child who is able to tolerate and grow stronger and not let terrible, terrible people weaken him. However, most children of permissive or uninvolved parents can be selfish, immature, dependent, unpopular, and lack social skills. There is a powerful saying that has continued to resonate with me for quite a while: "If you raise your children, you can spoil your grandchildren; but if you spoil your children, you'll have to raise your grandchildren."

Now, enter the perfect parent: Mrs. Authoritative. Note that now it is "authoritative" and not "authoritarian." "Authoritative" is a word that would commonly be used to describe George Washington, while "authoritarian" is a word that would commonly be used to describe an authoritarian regime. Mrs. Authoritative effectively combines both firm limits with affection and appreciation. Boundaries and limits are explicitly explained; mutual understanding and reason is sought after and achieved. There will be none of the "because I told you so" or "my house, my rules" stuff. Punishments are non-physical while aim to promote healthy behavior, and best only enacted occasionally for absolutely outrageous behaviors. Rewarding good behavior is common but not too common, which would make good behaviors only superficial in nature. Her children will understand rules, ethics, and love.

I believe that there are seven things that teenagers (and adults, and babies, and honestly, most everyone) need to be shown and given: 1) love, 2) positive truth, 3) respect, 4) non-transactional gratitude, 5) empiricism, 6) unconditional positive regard, and 7) "the blank check of trust." Parents love their children, but they need to show it. Open affection and love (not too public) is necessary to show kids that they can open up to others and give and receive positive energy. Positive truth ensures that neither party is simply pleasing the other, but rather working together to make sure both parties grow and benefit. In other words, you can be honest about your own feelings of disappointment in a constructive manner. Respect shows tolerance and acceptance, necessary for everyone to learn and necessary for every interaction. Gratitude makes sure that we stay connected to both the soil below and the heavens above. It allows us to appreciate what we have and not let our heads inflate or our hearts deflate. But gratitude should be non-transactional —it isn't saying "you should be grateful for what I do for you, Jimmy"; it's about teaching appreciation of everything as a blessing. I feel that I am blessed every morning to rise from my own bed and see my own family. I feel blessed to have fresh air and water and the opportunity to learn. Empiricism is the idea of learning by doing, as opposed to rationalism, or learning by reason or listening to what somebody else tells you. People will never learn to appreciate rationalism unless they are allowed to experience empiricism and make mistakes. And allowing teens to make their own mistakes without harsh judgement will enable them to accept themselves, accept parents, accept parents' mistakes, and understand that people are not perfect, and that is okay. We all start out as little scientists, don't we? I know it's scary, but that's where the next two things come in: unconditional positive regard and the blank check of trust.

You shouldn't love your kid because he or she got a good grade; you should love your kid simply because he or she is your kid. Unconditional positive regard leads to healthy development, whereas conditional positive regard leads to a great disparity between the real self and the ideal self, which causes incongruence.

And now, the blank check of trust... I call it that because it is literally a blank check of trust. It is letting teenagers sometimes live their own lives. It is the hardest thing to give a person, especially if you have experienced betrayal in your life. But everyone deserves a chance at it.

Now I know parents want the best for their kids and are therefore always worried. "What if independence or the blank check of trust or empiricism is a bad thing? Aren't my kids gonna be corrupt?" They may get hurt. But no, they will not corrupt, not if you truly taught them to be their own person with the values of kindness and truth. Parents hold the literal legal power. Therefore, they hold the responsibility. I know some babies keep crying and pooping seemingly without end in sight, and sometimes teenagers do that too. But if we are patient and open, we will learn tolerance from such and make a better future together.

I have to apologize for my large rant about parents. I understand that I am a teenager, and perhaps may have "no experience" in the minds of parents. But I believe that I have a well-thought-out perspective of a teenager.

Before we continue onto other adult relationships, I would like to emphasize something. Love, truth, respect, gratitude, empiricism, trust, and unconditional positive regard are not just things parents need to show or give their offspring—they are things you need to give yourself, too. Once you love yourself, once you tell yourself the positive truth, once you respect yourself (and etcetera because my fingers are tired from typing and you sure as hell don't want to hear me repeat the same seven words), then you will be the best resource for yourself and for others.

Finally, I believe that we are all babies and we are all adults. We innately have childlike innocence and childlike curiosity but also adultlike maturity and adultlike tolerance. We naturally care for people and are cared for by others. Except for babies, who stay babies until they learn the concept of how to be an adult and are strong enough to actually care for others. Anyway, there are going to be difficult "adults" and difficult "babies" out there in the world who are frustrating to deal with—in the workplace, in the classroom, and especially in the bathroom. But no matter who is around us, we have to seek understanding of others. People do not think about "what if" or "why" enough in society. That is why we have difficult adults raising difficult babies in endless cycles. Maybe from now on, we should look out for ourselves and look out for others.

I walk into the room, not because I have to, but because I just feel like it. And besides, I like to have conversations with many different people. I'm a high school student soon to graduate. And I trust this person with loads of life advice. It's my honors chemistry teacher from almost two years back.

You see, I was considering driving down to Maryland to visit colleges over the summer and the first thing Mrs. Spath told me was "Don't. From Albany to Baltimore area, the drive takes forever, and the gas cost just isn't worth it. *Trust* me. Fly out from Albany International and land in Baltimore-Washington. Cost is around the same, but the time saved is absolutely worth it."

I love to talk with not only teenagers but also teachers, administrators, staff, parents, and kids. We are not defined by our occupations; we are defined by our stories. And I believe every story is worth listening to. A lot of students think that all that matters is passing the class and getting out the door as quickly as possible. If I only paid attention to learning chemical formulas in Mrs. Spath's class, I wouldn't be where I am today. She knows so much about day-to-day tricks, the economy, and especially *iCarly*. She gave me driving advice and taught me how all interstate highways travelling north and south are odd numbered and all highways travelling east and west are even numbered. That was especially helpful a few days before my permit test.

I talk to my psychology teacher, Mr. Ferguson, about the counterculture movement - turn on, tune in, drop out! I talk to my history teacher, Mr. Rounds, about paintings and gargoyles and how I really like *Watson and the Shark* by James Singleton Copley because it shows the pure vulnerability of man.[7] I hide pranks in my biology teacher's room (don't tell Mrs. Babic!). I talk to my calculus teacher Mrs. Mahmood about... oatmeal. She insists that her steel-cut recipe is better than my instant oatmeal, but I've yet to have the effort to make it in the mornings.

John Singleton Copley: *Watson and the Shark*. Collection of the National Gallery of Art, Washington, D.C.

I like talking. My psychology teacher originally thought I was a brownnoser. Then, he told me, he realized that I just "really like sharing a bit too much." I can't teach you how to be a brownnoser, but I can teach you how to develop a genuine connection with both the content and the teacher of each class.

Everything you put out needs to be pure, positive energy. Anything less might as well be a waste. If you're only in school for the grade, then you've learned very little and will lack a lot when it comes to the real world. I'm not saying we have to spend hours learning material or get it all right, but we've just gotta have a good attitude about what we learn. Additionally, if we only talk to the teachers for the grade, then you miss out on a lot of very important interpersonal skills. More than anything, we need to be kind and compassionate to all from all walks of life. Learn something unique about the people around you. I use the example of teachers because I think it is the most applicable form of adult interaction for most students. However, we need to be kind and open and receptive to everyone, including fellow students and those younger than you. And once we give positive energy, we receive it back with other blessings and opportunities. People are always willing to help you if you are willing to learn.

When talking with an abundance of like- and different-minded people, you learn how to communicate in versatile and different, complementary ways. It's the same as making jokes about soccer with your soccer friends. It's the same as making ridiculous calculus jokes with your math classmates because you're all nervous wrecks and none of you have any idea what you're doing. That's flexing your personality. The environment affects your behavior, and your behavior begins to compliment the environment. Do the same thing with everyone, but do it on topics that those people actually care about. Yes, my pre-calculus teacher, Mrs. Turner, loves pre-calculus, but she also likes jigsaw puzzles and *Game of Thrones*. My statistics teacher, Mr. Letzring, love statistics and board games. His brother is one of the creators of Letiman Games! Go check them out!

Adolescence is a time where egocentrism is still quite prevalent. Teenagers often feel that nobody else could ever understand what they're going through. But everyone around us has also walked down the path of life. We are all unique, and so is a teenager's story, but that doesn't mean that we cannot learn from what others have to say.

However, I find a problem with adults sometimes. I feel as if they often raise themselves above teenagers in a silly way that is more than just age or seniority. To be completely honest, some adults are not any better than some teenagers. I have met meaner, more immature, and more closed-minded adults than my teenage friends and rivals. I have seen adults emotionally manipulate. I have seen adults disrespect entire livelihoods of other people. But again, we cannot do anything about how others behave; we can only act at our best. We have to hope that others are not fixated to early stages in life and are willing to grow.

Pawn Stars showrunner Rick Harrison was offered one of the rarest Pokémon card collections ever. The point of his show and his pawn shop is to identify good deals and make profits. While his assistant, Chum, immediately realized that the collection was valuable and most certainly worth bargaining, Rick took a different approach. His first question was, "It's like, a game, like, eight-year-old kids play, right?"[8] Off the bat, his demeanor is condescending and tries to paint a picture that the client is immature or foolish. He shows absolutely no healthy communication nor respect in the way he talks. He constantly calls it "Pokeman" despite being corrected constantly by Chum. This is a common tactic where, by calling it consistently the incorrect name without listening to others, the speaker asserts dominance despite having the least amount of knowledge and simultaneously demeans the subject at hand as "trivial." He is showing that his lack of knowledge "does not mean that he is unknowledgeable," but rather that the general population would consider Pokémon a "waste of time." Nonetheless, Rick takes an immature, closed-minded, and condescending way to deal with something in which he has no experience. He is looking for external validation as a strong and powerful person because he feels threatened. This is just as bad, if not worse, than some teenagers.

The most important thing is, despite the fact that different age groups have different cultures, beliefs, and cohort differences, we are not insensitive like Rick Harrison. We especially need to be sensitive towards our aging parents. In the movie *Un Padre No Tan Padre* (promoted in English as *From Dad to Worse*), 85-year-old Don Servando Villegas gets kicked out of his retirement home for being a cranky nuisance. A conservative Mexican patriarch (and bad, *authoritarian* and *permissive neglectful* parent) with no place to stay, he has to live with his youngest estranged son,

Francisco, the only one willing to take him in. Don Servando Villegas soon realizes that Francisco has a son, has a girlfriend (who is not the mother of the son), and has pot-smoking minority and homosexual roommates in a big house that they all share. Throughout hilarious scenes, Don Servando goes through a journey of realizing that values and culture change, and that he needs to open up and respect what the youth believes. Being close-minded will not get him, or anyone else, anywhere. When Francisco's girlfriend refuses to believe that he has changed, he says something very, very profound:

> DON SERVANDO. Déjame decirte algo. Cuando llegas a mi edad, vas a ver lo difícil que es… no sabes lo que se sientes ver que ya no eres indispensable para nadie.
>
> *Let me tell you something. When you reach my age, you'll see how difficult it is… you don't know how hard it is to know that nobody needs you anymore.*[9]

Most people don't want to change. And most people, just like Don Servando, especially do not want to hear people tell them to change. I know this is hypocritical coming from a book, but I do believe one way in which we could all change is to really put ourselves in other peoples' shoes. One day I will be old, estranged from the technology of the future and with friends who probably will never be able to travel to see me. I hope people will still care about me when I can no longer swim, or run, or walk, or stand. I hope people can understand that I am from a different time, a different world. I hope I can keep up with the values of the future without feeling that the world has lost its integrity, something that almost every aging person questions today. I hope people will respect us when we have gray hair; and I hope that we still have the heart to respect people even when our minds fade.

Most people don't want advice. People don't want to hear that their ways are wrong, or that their values are invalid. People feel attacked when new or better information is given. But we, you and I, don't need to be weakened or feel lesser when we learn from others. Because we can learn from anyone.

> FRANCISCO. No estar de acuerdo con lo que alguien trae en la mente no significa que no puedes aprender de lo que lleva en el corazón.
>
> *Not agreeing with what's in someone's mind doesn't mean you can't learn from what's in their heart*

CHAPTER 7

Diversity, Unity, and Respect

THIS IS THE CHAPTER that I was most concerned about writing. Throughout my childhood and teenage years, I developed my own sense of what identity means (or should mean) in society. However, I, just like many others, am afraid to openly discuss race and gender because they are "touchy subjects." But we must discuss them. "Touchy subjects" should never be sugarcoated or concealed in society, or else we risk repressing or neglecting our own identities. I would like to take you through my opinion of what diversity, unity, and respect are to me.

I think debates about gender and race necessary, but they often end up toxic or volatile. They are volatile because these arguments are more emotional in nature simply due to the significance of personal identity; and there is often a component of perceived threat, fear, or hatred. While such is totally understandable, it leads many to take defensive or offensive attacking stances that do not release positive truth or positive energy. Then again, hatred and discrimination have existed throughout history, which is why it is hard today to simply have everyone take a high road... some of us feel rightfully angry. It is hard to promote kindness while also fighting for yourself. But that is exactly what we need to learn.

Why do people get offended? I believe that there are two main paths. If I said something disrespectful, someone else can reasonably be offended. If I said something with respect or with positive truth, then it is the other person who wants to make it a problem. Topics on race and gender are so sketchy because the difference between the two paths is very obscure, ambiguous, and individualized. When it comes to speaking up about gender or race, it seems as if only the first person who started speaking could ever be blamed or ever be in the wrong, because the recipients always have the option to be offended or pretend to be offended, hiding under the curtain of victimization. But, let us ease gradually before getting analytical.

My name is Juneau. My parents were born in China. I was born in Boston. As a child, other kids would ask me tons of questions: Why are your eyes so tiny? Is this the Chinese middle finger? Kids would also assert a few facts to me: You look like my other friend. You two must be cousins.

Your name doesn't sound Asian. You are definitely not from Boston.

Sometimes, I feel that children are not little scientists. They are little bastards. Hahah, kidding. Anyway, to be completely honest, I didn't really mind. And I have no spite towards children because they are children. Children have an innate curiosity but are also egocentric. They do not have an innate empathetic understanding of how their words may disrespectfully release accusative or negative energy towards others. That is something that we all have to learn.

Fast forward to today. Again, my name is Juneau. But substitute teachers sometimes call me Josh, Kevin, Jason, or the name of any other Asian that is in my grade. However, at least they aren't asking why my eyes are so tiny (it's actually my eyelids that are tiny, not my eyeballs).

I'm gonna be honest again. I know I shouldn't be laughing when people make mistakes, but I find it kinda funny. I think I am used to it, and there's a part of me that probably could get mad, but I let it go. There is something scientifically known as the cross-race effect. There exists a natural tendency for someone to more easily recognize faces of the race with which he or she is most familiar. If you grow up in a white community with a white family, you'll have a harder time distinguishing between Asian people. All races also have more difficulty recognizing and interpreting the facial and emotional expressions of other races.[1] We are naturally better at identifying individuals of our own race and naturally worse at identifying individuals of other races. I am sure we have all made mistakes before, so we shouldn't hold it over anyone else's head. Nobody needs to get butthurt when someone makes a genuine mistake as long as that someone is willing to learn from the mistake.

This is where respect comes in. We have all got to be willing to learn and willing to be kind before we attack or label someone as sexist or racist. And we have to respect all those around us of all walks of life. Like I said a few chapters back, we humans are very quick to assume negative intentions from peoples' actions or words before we even try to ask or understand. We have to stop jumping to conclusions.

However, people often jump to conclusions about me. A natural survival instinct, people create heuristics, practical "rules of thumb" that some or most of the time are "true." Humans are also visual creatures, and gauge their beliefs based on what they see. Connect heuristics to superficial characteristics and you get racial stereotypes of people who are unlike you. Once formed, it is very difficult to get rid of stereotypes. Most humans associate socioeconomic status, intelligence, and other characteristics simply based on race.

People think I'm docile. They soon learn that I most certainly am not. People like to think I like Chinese food. I actually like Maine lobster more (although I've always wanted to try rock lobster!). People think I'm good at math.

I'd like to think this is true, but you should confer with my math teachers.

Again, heuristics are rules of thumb that are sometimes correct. Do Asian people usually like Asian food? Yes. Are Asian people usually taught to be more orderly and less loud than Americans? Yes. Do Asian students usually play an instrument in the orchestra? Yes. Are Asian students usually good at math? Yes.

I don't bother trying to change peoples' heuristics when they are generally true. However, it does very much bother me when people believe stereotypes are true of a whole race, or that race causes socioeconomic or intellectual qualities, or that, because of certain general qualities, some races are better than others. Such reflects an inability or unwillingness to understand or respect those who are different from you.

I don't give two shits if children ask me about the Chinese middle finger. I don't give two shits if adults call me by the wrong name sometimes. I do give two shits, however, when someone says that I am good at math because I am Asian. I do give two shits when people tell me I want to be a doctor simply because my parents forced me to. Why doesn't anyone try to believe that I grew up loving learning? Why doesn't anyone try to believe that I grew up genuinely wanting to help others?

America believes that Asian-Americans are quiet, hard workers who earn a lot of money and don't go out in public that often. I have heard fellow Asians say something that really bothers them… they feel as if, in America, they can become successful enough, but they will never be at the top because they are Asian. I don't share this sentiment, but you can see that society creates socioeconomic barriers on race that can affect the way that people perceive other races and their own.

One of the ways that I feel Asians are most impacted is in the perception of beauty in the English world. To this day in America, Asian features are not considered the beauty ideal. And I have seen many white people, including some of my friends, struggle with the idea of even sharing a romantic connection with someone of another race. And I see it in the way some white girls talk to me. People find it hard to ever become intimate with someone of another race.

A friend and I both discovered what it meant to be ourselves in eighth grade. At that time, I was struggling with my own identity, and trying to understand how I was supposed to act, and in what parts of myself should I take pride or shame. My friend is half black and half white. We both felt as if white people could not understand our struggles. She gave me comfort and made me feel like I could be appreciated and loved despite my race. She taught me that I should never take shame in any part of myself. Our acceptance of each other made me become stronger and let me learn to accept myself and love myself for who I am. We were both different, and we had fought in different ways to get where we are today. Lia, I am always wishing you the best.

I used to make fun of my own ethnicity. I think a lot of Asian teens do that, because it makes people laugh and it's a shortcut to temporarily make yourself feel accepted. I know an adult who still jokes about himself and others being Asian. But that is a fixation. We need to get over it and realize that people are not defined by their race. We cannot define or treat ourselves, nor others, based off of a long string of "sometimes true" assumptions related to superficial characteristics.

Now, gender. I am a man. I am a guy. I am also straight, and like girls way too much to be gay. But can guys sing? Are guys allowed to dance or do musicals? These were the questions that ran through my mind in the first few years of high school. I discovered my race identity but I was still worried about my gender identity. From the heuristic of males in musicals and shows, I was afraid of being viewed as gay, not because being gay is a bad thing, but simply because I wanted people to know and believe that I like girls because I *really really* like girls. But then I realized something. I know that I am a guy. I know that I really really like girls. I know that I love to sing. Why does what other people think matter? Why does what society expects of a male student athlete matter? Once I had confidence in my voice and love for myself, I went back onto the stage for the first time in five years. In summary, who gives a shit about what others say? Do what you want and be who you are. There is a quote from Bernard Baruch, presidential advisor to Franklin Delano Roosevelt, that is often misattributed to Dr. Seuss: "Those who mind don't matter and those who matter don't mind."[2]

If that were micro-touchy-subjects, now I would like to talk about macro-touchy-subjects. From my perspective, there is an inherent safety hazard with the way that we talk about race or gender in the big picture. Whereas appreciation of diversity can and should be used in a respectful, unifying way, it often is used paradoxically as a divisive technique, deliberately creating hostile environments for different ingroups to non-constructively attack each other.

I believe in diversity and what it can be.

I believe that it is totally okay and absolutely encouraged to identify with your identity and with who you are. I am a proud American and a proud New Englander living in New York. I have been a die-hard New England Patriots fan since the day I was born that Saturday afternoon in 2002. Social identity, or the understanding of to whom we belong, is absolutely important. Additionally, so is our reference group, or to whom we compare. I am a teenager in New York with Asian heritage (social identity) in a country full of teenagers (reference group) that I compare myself to.

It is natural and perfectly fine to create ingroups. However, what is not fine is hostility, unkindness, and disrespect towards outgroups. Yet often, we promote our own ingroup by deliberately putting down other people. The emotional rouse and struggle for equality is not always constructive. For example, Anaïs Nin, a French-Cuban American writer and profound feminist, is quoted as saying "I hate men who are afraid of women's strength." We understand the logic behind her statement, but the emotion and heart is in a spiteful place. The use of the words "hate" and "afraid" suggest negative emotion and conflict. In fact, every action is negative in this instance. Her words are meant to emotionally rouse women into fighting for their own rights by making it look like an "us-them" scenario. Advocating for rights is good, but negative emotions are not. In reality, we need to be a totally progressive society, where there is emphasis on cooperation and the idea that we will all be better off if we actively help the individuals.

I understand that disenfranchised people feel frustration and anger, I have been one of them. But we cannot turn that anger into division. We need to respect and turn that anger into unity and peaceful protest. On Twitter, I see many people say "I hate men, men are trash, I'm sick of men."[3] Feminism is meant to be the promotion of equality. Proponents of hatred will destroy the entire cause. Same with "I hate white people." If you want to screw around and make jokes, then whatever. If you actually want to make a change towards equality, then you need to stop thinking that this is a battle between two divided sides.

We also need to focus on the serious matters when it comes to advocating for equality. No, it is not racist if someone assumes I speak Chinese (I actually speak Spanish). No, it is not sexist when somebody says "grow a pair." It was racist when blacks in America were imposed poll taxes by the white elite to economically prevent them from voting. It is racist when my classmates say that I am good at music because all Asians are good at music. It was sexist when women were denied good jobs in the public workplace. It is sexist when my classmates openly say that men are trash.

My great-grandmother was the daughter of a high-ranking official in the Qing Dynasty court. What makes the Qing Dynasty different from previous dynasties is that the Qing Dynasty rulers are not of Han Chinese ethnicity. The Qing Dynasty was Manchu. We have a slightly different look than the Han Chinese; my mother always felt "different" as a kid. We also inherited generations of value of equality.

Before Mao Zedong promoted that "women hold half the sky,"[4] and before the Qing Dynasty, foot binding still persisted throughout China. The Han elite believed that all proper ladies should have cute, tiny [nonfunctional] feet. It was a terrible tradition. The Manchu Qing Dynasty tried to ban it multiple times. My Manchu ancestors did not footbind. My great-grandmother learned how to box, how to swordfight, and how to ride a horse. My mother did parkour and defended herself and her sister from thieves and bullies. My mother has never doubted that she is equal to men.

Now, I want to talk about equality in America, but this is where it gets "touchy." Forgive my expressions, in my opinion, at least sometimes, boys are dumb, and girls are idiots. Sometimes, boys are incapable of doing things they want to do. Sometimes, girls sabotage things they make. That is how we are raised in America. Here's why.

Generations pass down their ideas about how each gender should act through activities, speech, behavior, and other subtle ways. Nobody ever directly tells boys to be dumbass douchebags who play sports and take tons of stupid risks. And likewise, nobody ever directly tells girls to follow the rules, be subordinate, and have low self-esteem. We get these ideas subconsciously from our parents. The best feeling for a father is when he takes his sons out to watch a ball game or to play football in the backyard. The best feeling for a mother is when she teaches her daughters to dress up or to learn their formal table manners. From the get-go, American boys discover the id and learn about sports, independence, and taking risks, while American girls discover the superego and learn about appearance, cooperation, makeup, and following the rules.

Collectively, society believes that boys are boys and girls are girls. Boys will be reckless, girls will be ruly. Boys will be independent, girls will be collective. Teenage boys lack social manners and do not care what other boys do. Teenage girls advocate manners and become angry at other girls who do not follow manners, but will not use violence or directness (things that boys are taught) to scold the unruly girls. Rather, teenage girls will use passive-aggressiveness and emotional manipulation.

After having been a captain of the boys varsity swimming and diving team for two years, and having cooperated with the girls team, I have noticed one major difference. When girls get mad at each other, they badmouth behind backs and sabotage. When guys get mad at each other, they strip naked and fight it right there and then. For personal preference, I am happy that I am on the boys team. Pick your poison.

You see these values sometimes fixate in adults. For example, I know many men who value sports yet see absolutely no value in the arts. I know many women who use passive-aggressive techniques and emotional manipulation. The result is that guys are unable to learn or comprehend anything out of their current mental models, and that girls lack self-esteem due to sabotage and pettiness.

Go on Instagram. Find a guy who has a specific amount of followers. Find a girl who has around the same amount of followers. Then, go to their most recent posts. The guy will almost always have fewer likes than the girl. The guy will have no comments on his post, while the girl will have millions of comments that say "so pretty" or "adorable" or "dayumn bbygrl." Girls are taught this value to support each other, even if it's disingenuine, while guys are taught this value of strong independence and stemming support of each other. Guys will punch your teeth out and won't apologize for it. Girls will spread rumors about you being a slut and pretend it wasn't them.

I don't have a solution for this. We can't just magically ask every dad to teach their sons how to cook or teach every mom to teach their daughters how to play football. As long as culture and values exist, the disappearance of these inherent "differences" will be almost impossible. I do believe in one thing, however... educated men and women are more effective and less polarized members of society. Smart men do not have to follow toxic masculinity because they are smart, and guys don't deal with them. Smart women do not have to follow toxic femininity because they are smart, and girls don't deal with them.

I'm going to be honest. Biology exists and is unchanging. Saying "I can't see color" or "I can't see sex" is a neglectful stance that pretends like differences don't exist. What we need to recognize is that biology is inherent, and that racism and sexism and the feeling of self-disenfranchisement are not; and that we must promote general respect and kindness if we want society to progress. Women get to be picky about the men they like because they are the child bearers and their goal is to ensure that their offspring are the fittest, but that doesn't mean they can stomp on men.

Men get to be... men can pass themselves around more because their goal is to simply ensure that they have offsprings, but that doesn't mean they can cheat on their partners. Men will (or should) naturally give women flowers and hold open the door for them, not because they think women are weak or flowery, but because they want to be kind people; and women should accept these gestures with reciprocated positive energy. However, when the man expects the woman to cook when they both have nine to five jobs... yeah, that's slightly one-sided. When people show respect, please show gratitude. When people show ignorance, know that karma will get them, we just can't hold it over their heads.

On that note, here are some skills that are stereotyped as one-sided that I believe both sexes should understand. Both sexes should learn how to cook, repair, clean, and fight. That is for your own quality of life. Self-sufficiency and having skill sets is a great way of making sure you feel confident in yourself and in control of your own life.

I want to quickly touch on those who are transgender or are homosexual. It's simple: I should not have any right or influence over who you want to be. You are who you are; love is love. You are a unique human, just like I am a unique human. Do whatever you want as long as you respect others different from you. I also want to touch on religion. It's simple: I should not have any right or influence over who you want to be. You are a unique human, just like I am a unique human. Do whatever you want as long as you respect others different from you.

Finally, this goes for all people of all walks of life. No matter what happens in front of you, never let yourself feel disenfranchised. The word "minority" does not mean that we are lesser. We always and unconditionally need to love ourselves and fight for our rights. It is harder to fight when some part of us thinks or believes that we are treated as lesser by others or are actually lesser than others. You are enough. We can never let ourselves be weakened by the words or actions of others. We will stay strong and fight the right battles with compassion and kindness.

When I was in ninth grade, I didn't realize this yet. I was in my world history class, and we were learning about foot binding. I couldn't bear to look at the presentation nor at the faces around me. And then the girl in front of me, known for being both progressive in terms of rights but also overbearing, whispered something to the girl next to her that I quickly heard: "I bet the Chinese invented the wheelchair as well." That was the first time I ever felt personally attacked. Someone was both simultaneously making fun of our intelligence and the shameful and controversial aspects of our past culture. I went up to my teacher after class, and she said something that I still remember. She told me that she's tried to change that student many times, but that student is unwilling to learn and unwilling to change. But even in my most vulnerable state, my teacher believed that I was strong, kind, and compassionate. She trusted that I could take the negative energy thrown at me, and rather than throw it anywhere, let it dissolve. She trusted that I could take the high road and use kindness and compassion and respect even when those around me didn't. I learned from my teacher's amazing and huge heart. And I believe in you. I believe you can take the high road, even in your darkest moments. I believe in you because somebody believed in me.

I don't like it when people talk openly about how Asians eat cats and dogs or when people discuss the Rape of Nanjing. But I don't let it attack me and I don't let it lessen me. I need to be kind, no matter what; and we should, as a society, always try to teach others to cleanse the worst illness that is ignorance. I am not afraid of stereotypes or of how people look at me. My life isn't mine if I always care about what others think.

When it comes to anyone, every interaction is an opportunity to learn. We have to make respect our North Star and compassion our compass. We always have the choice to take the best from the best and to make the best from the worst. We cannot divide ourselves by the color of our skin or the gender by which we adhere. But conversely, we cannot neglect it either. The universe blesses us with life and with biological incidence, but it also blesses us with the ability to mold our own destinies. We need to promote diversity, but we also need to promote unity. We should be a united human race, a vessel of light sailing in the night sky.

Rembrandt van Rijn: *The Storm on the Sea of Galilee*.
Collection of the Isabella Stewart Gardner Museum,
Boston; Stolen in 1990.[5]

CHAPTER 8

Overcoming Adversity

DUSK MELTED into the dark night. I remember it. The sky was a dark blue, one of the darkest blues you could ever imagine. I was driving, my mother right next to me. Every day, we would drive through a wooded park, hushed by towering trees and flowing rivers. At the end of the park was always a long road that drove past tiny houses, surrounded by nothing but open, quiet fields.

The only lights were the moon, the stars, and the neighboring cell phone towers a few thousand meters away. But then, a sign lights up in front of us, as it does every night. I stop my car and put it into park a few hundred yards away from the sign. The sign burns red and moves its mechanical arms down to block the road in front of it. Every night there is an evening train that passes by. The train cars enter and exit my field of view faster than I can comprehend. The sound is loud and droning, but comforting and familiar.

After what seems like an eternity, but at the same time only ten seconds, the train disappears behind tall pines and the silence returns. The sign lifts up its arms and we continue driving, like we always do. But tonight was also a bit different.

I already knew that my parents were separating. I would be an idiot if I didn't. And I already knew that my mom had just visited her boyfriend in the hospital. But knowing and understanding are two different things.

I hold my mom's hand. She tells me about how they are divorcing, how she has always loved, and will always love, my father but no longer wants to be with him. She feels as if the two of them have been lacking something together for many years. She tells me that the divorce will be complicated, but that everything will work out in the end. I believe her.

Then she tells me about her boyfriend at the time. I really liked him. Nobody could ever replace my father to me, and her boyfriend didn't, because he was a completely different man and a completely new friend. He was bright and intelligent in his own ways. He loved the classics, he loved philosophy, and I loved discussing with him.

A few months earlier, he had his first open heart surgery. But the replacement valves got infected, and he needed to go again for a second operation. The first time, he didn't really care. He was not scared of anything. But the second time, he was afraid. He didn't want to die.

She continues talking to me. The second surgery was successful. His heart was working. But his brain was gone. He forgot how to speak, he forgot how to think. Nurses would have to strap him down and force feed him so he wouldn't starve. He only recognized one face: my mother's. And he only smiled when my mother said one of two things: "I love you," or "Juneau got the car. Juneau finally bought the car we were talking about."

I was in the neighborhood, driving back home, when I saw a rabbit run in front of me. I had no time to react, and it disappeared under the wheel of my car. I stopped the car. My vision became blurry. Then, I cried long and hard. I hadn't cried in ages. But after a few years, life got to me. I was thinking about the passing of my father's parents just the year before. I was thinking about how I felt bullied and fell out with my best friend. I was thinking about divorce. I was thinking about losing my mom's boyfriend. And I was thinking about how I probably just killed a rabbit. My mom opened the car door to check, and she promised me that I didn't kill the rabbit. That made me feel better, but I continued crying. For the first time in my life, I understood pure sadness. Darker and bluer than the night sky above me. Sadness isn't stubbing your toe or failing a test or arguing with a friend—sadness is divorce and death.

Overcoming Adversity

The hardest part about life is understanding that you can't change the bad things that have happened to you. We wish we could just roll back time and redo everything, but we can't. What is past has passed, we only have the present. We can only try to make the future better. We must change the things we cannot accept and accept the things we cannot change.

I have always had two beliefs, and throughout my darkest days I have stuck with them. When my friends and family are sad, I promise them these two beliefs, both crucial promises we must make to ourselves and to others. First, the universe never gives us more than we can handle. Second, life gets better and its path ends well. I now want to talk about some of my inspirations.

Mrs. Kelly Babic is the absolute best example of what it means to put your all into what you do. I had the honor of having her as a teacher twice—once for Honors Biology, again for AP Biology. She creates presentations and complimentary note sheets that are in-depth and highly exhaustive of what she is asked to teach for her classes. She is straightforward and communicative; Mrs. Babic makes sure that all students in her class are able to succeed as long as they put the work in. She is enthusiastic, kind, and she loves biology… I remember her face lighting up when my lab group caught our first water flea. I remember her joy when we were able to slow down the heartbeat of our first water flea. I remember her excitement when we were able to speed up the heartbeat of our second water flea. And I absolutely remember her astonishment (and our entire class's curiosity) when we accidentally caught a humongous aquatic insect. She has an innate passion for biology and living beings.

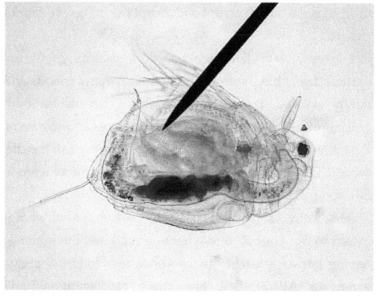

Daphnia (water flea) under a microscope with a clear exoskeleton and heart. Also with a filled digestive tract.

In the beginning of my junior year, Mrs. Babic was wearing a medical boot and had a knee scooter. She badly injured her lower leg after falling down the stairs a few days before school started. She would need to have surgery and would be out for a few weeks the first few months of school. But I don't ever remember her being negative... she would call her scooter her "scoot-scoot" and would just continue "scooting on with life." And even at home, while she was recovering, she continued to upload message plans, grade papers, and communicate with us.

Mrs. Babic does it all. When she teaches, when she takes care of her kids, when she is faced with obstacles, she constantly puts out positive energy. She is the reason that I want to study biology in the future. But more importantly, she showed me that we are not defined by our adversities, but rather by how we overcome them.

Mrs. Durray Mahmood has been a mentor to me not only in AP Calculus but also in life. Leaving Pakistan, she and her husband left their homes, their families, their stables sources of income, and everything that they knew. They wanted to secure a better life for their children, travelling across the world for work, for education, and most importantly, to find a safe home. From Saudi Arabia, to Italy, to England, to Australia, they constantly ventured outside of Pakistan, working hard and with passion. At times it was difficult, with one parent in school and the other trying to find work to support their four children. They finally came to the United States with the diversity program lottery visa before the turn of the new century. Mrs. Mahmood began teaching at my high school in 2000. Since then, she has always been dedicated in preparing her students for college and for their futures. But after September 11th of 2001, people changed their perspectives on the Islamic faith. Fear blackened minds to anger. Long-time teachers stopped showing as much appreciation or respect for Mrs. Mahmood. One day, Mrs. Mahmood put her bag in the middle of the table in the faculty room. Another teacher was also in the faculty room. Mrs. Mahmood went to make copies of papers in the adjacent copier room. When she returned, her bag and its contents were scattered across the floor. She was never able to find her school planner.

But honestly, that isn't the part of the story that Mrs. Mahmood likes to emphasize. She wanted to let me know that, no matter what happened, her students were always kind to her. She did not let the bad weaken her. To this day, she is grateful for how her neighbors, her students, and how other teachers treated her with kindness. She looks for the good in life. Mrs. Mahmood has the kindest heart, strongest attitude, and greatest compassion towards all.

Many years later, she fell while in her classroom, tripping over a misplaced electric fan. She tore her rotator cuff and needed to be sent to the hospital. Not only did she try to come back to school the next day to continue teaching, she also personally thanked every single teacher, student, and nurse that helped her get medical attention. No matter what happens, she always smiles and has the finest sense of humor (she and I talk both about furthering Calculus knowledge and Seth Meyers jokes).

Mrs. Mahmood believes as children, we should all live for our parents. We should grow up healthy and safe and beautiful so that our parents can forever see us alive and well. And when we have kids of our own, we should live for them and care for them. And Mrs. Mahmood's children are now grown up, young and healthy adults, so she says she now lives for and cares for her students.

Mrs. Mahmood one afternoon told me that she never wants to retire because she finds the greatest joy in teaching. I was on the verge of tears. Mrs. Mahmood has not only self-actualized, but she is happy. She is grateful for all the blessings in her life and gives love and support to those around her. I believe there is much to learn from people like Mrs. Mahmood. I know not where my life path will bring me, but I know that I must be a good person, I must love what I do, and I must love those around me.

I hope that I have taken you on an emotional journey throughout this chapter. What my teachers' experiences and my own experience have taught me is that we need to keep going. We can never give up on ourselves. Mrs. Babic and Mrs. Mahmood are some of the most resilient people that I have ever met. And they came into my life at a time when I needed it most. Again, staying positive is not bottling up or denying the negative emotions inside your soul; staying positive is simply not allowing those negative emotions to taint your entire life.

I have my ups and downs. I don't hide them or cover them up. Throughout every experience, I let myself feel the emotions within me. And if I need to, I cry. It is absolutely okay to cry. But when the sun rises the next morning and I'm blessed to see it, I know that I need to continue onward.

If we fixate on the bad things in life, then we miss out on the good things. We need to appreciate each living and breathing moment for what it is. The traffic commute should never affect how much we liked hanging out with our friends.

I think the biggest frustration for a lot of people is dealing with time. Life is both the shortest and longest experience which we all share together. We feel as if we don't have enough time to do everything that we want to do. We feel as if life goes too slowly or too quickly, each bad moment too long and each good moment too short. But the thing is, we cannot control time and we cannot control what happens in our lives. We have to trust that the path will get better and lead to a happy ending, and then work towards it.

Time also is thrown the blame when it comes to finding a partner. We feel as if that person would've been the right person for us "if only it were at a different time." We constantly feel as if circumstance or time takes us away from perfect people. However, we need to understand that, if time and circumstance are unwilling, then it is not the right person for us. When we find the right person, it will genuinely be the right person. Time and circumstance will beckon together to show us where our path is meant to be.

Overcoming Adversity

Throughout my life, I have always blindly trusted the universe. I am willing to let it show me the path and tell me what I need to do. Juju Chang, former anchor of ABC's *Good Morning America* and current anchor of *Nightline*, told me and my mother something extremely important: "You can do everything that you want, just not all at the same time." We need to put faith in the fact that the future only gets better, and that the future is in our hands. I might be a student now, but someday, I hope that the world may hear my songs about how we are all connected even though we may not speak the same language. Then, I hope you may find my name among the scientists seeking to rectify debilitating illnesses that have affected my friends and family. Circumstance and time may not allow me to do all at the same time, but it surely will not stop me. The struggle against time and circumstance is exactly what makes us human.

Please believe in yourself. I believe in you. We can never give up.

George Frederic Watts: *Hope*. Collection of Tate Britain, London.[1]

CHAPTER 9

Honesty and Making Mistakes

I BELIEVE TRUE HAPPINESS requires one very important action: we must accept everything about ourselves. But to a lot of people, this seems counterintuitive. We are all flawed human beings and we make mistakes often. How the hell can we accept everything and then also be happy? This was most certainly paradoxical for me for ages, but two humongous mistakes changed the way that I feel about happiness. *Common* "happiness" is ignoring your mistakes... *true* happiness is accepting them.

To be completely honest, *nobody ever wants to hear the truth*. But how am I going to write a chapter on "Honesty and Making Mistakes" if I don't write about the truth? I need to warn you now—I will not be politically correct this chapter. This chapter can be potentially offensive and depending on your perspective, it could be hurtful. This is going to be a lot to swallow for all of us, so please know that I emphasize both kindness and positive truth, but right now we have to focus on the unfiltered and harsh truth.

People often say that history repeats itself. That is because we humans fall under the false impression that common happiness, the one without the acknowledgement of the positive truth, is satisfactory. I believe that such in our minds should be anything but satisfactory.

Let's pretend that there's a teenage young woman who is very reckless, Ms. Reckless. She loves humor and values it more than kindness. Don't get me wrong, she is very kind to her friends. However, Ms. Reckless does not treat people the same way. She bitches a lot. She laughs a lot, probably more than I do, but she never feels like she has enough. Every aching second, she wishes to be out with her friends. Ms. Reckless cannot be alone. And when she wants to be funny, sometimes she doesn't think about what she says, and she hurts one of her friend's feelings. She then realizes it, feels bad about it, apologizes, and then moves on. But her values never change. She still values humor more than kindness, thus continues to repeat the cycle. Her happiness is common happiness.

Let's pretend that there's a teenage young man who is very stubborn, Mr. Stubborn. He loves it when he is viewed as a kind person by others. He wants no one to think that he is anything but kind. Mr. Stubborn gets a lot of compliments and praise, much more than I do, but he never feels like he has enough. Every aching second, he wishes to be out with his friends. Mr. Stubborn cannot be alone. Sometimes, his desire for attention causes him to seem as if he neglects others or is trying to take the spotlight. He has promised people things to make himself seem like a good friend, just to break them. But what happens when you mention a broken promise to him? If someone else did it, it's unfair and Mr. Stubborn can't believe anyone would do that to you. If he did it, he ignores your complaint. I have never heard him say the word "sorry" in a genuine context. But it doesn't matter, because he loves to be around his friends, and nobody would dare point this out except I. His happiness is common happiness.

Thank you for listening. I am truly sorry (and cringing at the fact) that I am being critical and blunt. I also want to say that I am good friends with, and love and accept these people. I'm sorry that I am pushing the emotional envelope by telling my truth, but I need to get to a point: neither of these people truly accept themselves for who they are. Therefore, neither of them is willing to learn or grow as a person.

This is where true happiness becomes counterintuitive. The defense mechanisms of the ego are completely naturally-occurring ways to neglect reality or the truth to make us feel better. Our ego, the midpoint between our innate desires and our self-denying attitudes, wants to be sheltered from harsh reality and from negative emotions. A sheltered ego arrives at "common happiness." But to be truly happy, we need to accept the entirety of reality. Once we do that, we finally realize how we can improve ourselves and the world around us.

I was not much better, let's be real. I wanted to seem smarter than everyone around me. That caused me to purposefully put people down. I also didn't care for those who weren't my friends. I wanted to teach people lessons based on my judgement. So rather than letting karma do its work, I would do it myself. At that time, I was fine with life. But two mistakes made me realize that my common happiness is not enough. In order for me to grow as a person and truly be happy, I needed to accept myself, even my bad parts.

There was a person who accepted me before I ever came close to accepting myself. She was one of my best friends in eighth grade. We would work on art projects together every week. It felt like an escape from the harshness of reality, a breath of relief that kept me moving forward. My guy friends didn't understand why I liked her so much... but nobody else has to understand the people and things that make you happy. I saw the kindest heart when I looked at her, and to this day that is all I see.

It was at this time that I started writing. I started writing my diary, I started writing short stories. And it was she who constantly motivated me to keep going. I would give her a story to read every single week. If she smiled, that was what mattered to me. She kept me going.

But then I started feeling as if we became more distant. I knew she started talking to this other guy. So, I let myself blame her for my dwindling personal motivation to keep writing. I asked her if she wanted to hang out outside of school, and she said yes. But then, she cancelled on me a few days before. Looking back on it now, I'm sure she had a valid reason to cancel. We were eighth graders. We shouldn't expect to always have control of our own lives. We couldn't drive, our parents were busy, the whole lot…

But I took it personally. I felt ignored or misunderstood since I had asked her first and obtained her agreement. I felt like she was betraying me. I felt like maybe she didn't care about me. I felt like I needed to teach her a lesson. I let my own hurt lash out onto the person who motivated me in a million ways. I shut her out of my life and did not accept her apology for many months. And when freshman year came around, sometimes I would make fun of her. It would be phrases I would say, mockingly, in public, that nobody else could understand but she.

I didn't think about this for a while. I felt like I was in the right. But then came the summer and I had to be away for an internship on my own for a long time. And I began to think… a lot. I believe that this is when I started truly thinking in my life. Thinking about myself, thinking about my actions, thinking about others. A few days before the solar eclipse of August 21, 2017, over a year and a half after our falling out, I knew I had to say something. I had to fix something that I had broken. I was done with arrogance, with "teaching people lessons." I sent her a message:

Lia,

I wanted to apologize for how weird and rude I was acting around this time last year. It still bothers me everyday how I treated you. I'm sorry.

I wanted to let you know that you were a really good friend. You pushed me to grow and to continue writing stories, and I draw most of that inspiration from you. It was because of you that I sent my stories to get published, and it was because of you that I continued writing. Thank you.

Sorry if this all came out of the blue. I wanted to clear this all up.

I wish you a prosperous future, and never forget that you can always change the world. You changed mine.

Best wishes,

Juneau

Honesty and Making Mistakes

I didn't know how I was supposed to talk to a friend that I felt I had lost. But I said what I wanted to say. And she responded with the kindest heart I have ever seen:

This meant the world to me. No worries Juneau. I understand why you were upset and I apologize as well and I'm glad we've cleared this up. Enjoy the rest of your summer.

How could someone be so understanding and so forgiving despite what I've done?

I no longer wanted to resist the waves of circumstance or cower under fear and shame by hiding myself under a hardening shell. I promised myself that someday I would only radiate positivity. I'm not there yet, but for Lia and for myself I am now sticking to that promise.

Unfortunately, I would forget about that promise until the end of my sophomore year. It's easy for someone to write a book about all the good things they want to show you. It's easy to showcase our best parts. But if we want honesty, I need to show you the bad as well.

I hosted a New Year's party my sophomore year. It was me and my six best guy friends, who I considered truly trustworthy and amazing people. No alcohol, no drugs, nothing illegal. We are probably the few who strictly disliked illegal substances from our high school. Anyway, my friend brought up this idea that his other friends had proposed to him earlier—a bracket. And I decided maybe it would be fun. We knew that girls would compare guys in their mind and guys would compare girls, so we thought it would be sick to make it a formal tournament. From a comprehensive perspective, we made a bracket of girls we knew from our school. It did not matter that the criteria we used in our minds were non-demeaning—we were comparing previous crushes and their personalities, how funny/nice they were to us, and we used academic and athletic excellence as criteria—but the outside world would have never known that. My friends and I were really just a bunch of funny, nerdy, righteous and idealistic dudes. All of us have parents and teachers who have high expectations of us, and we were, at least used to be, considered "good boys." We hosted the bracket, which was a list of names with different rounds of eliminations, on an online private server. To us, it was just a light and thoughtless (and idiotic) activity for half an hour before we moved onto other things, like making jigsaw puzzles and eating macaroni and cheese.

But somehow, that private server could be found by a simple Google search. And when something like that came into the eyes of classmates at our school, especially those within the bracket, people turned angry and expected the worst. That was the day that revealed the true colors of me and my friends.

Honesty and Making Mistakes

It was a Saturday morning. I remember seeing my own doing on the feeds of many social media, Instagram, Facebook, Twitter... I wanted to faint. Nobody ever wanted this to get out. And nobody ever wanted to hurt anyone. But obviously, people were hurt by it. People were enraged. People demanded to know who did this.

Before I tell you what happened next, please allow me to share with you what I felt then and now are quite different. I understood the consequences of my actions, and I also now learned to appreciate each of my friends' unique circumstances and concerns. So, I hope by sharing this story, you and they would understand me, as well as forgive me.

The bracket boiled over social media like bubbling lava. Before consulting with all of us, two of my friends immediately denied having done it. One of them said he'd do anything for us if the rest of us took the blame. The other publicly claimed that he and a third friend were never involved. Back then I concluded that none of them wanted to get into any trouble or to be discovered by their parents or the school—now I simply feel their views and perspectives might have been different than mine. So, three people who actually had done it had already denied. The problem with this is that it led people to begin to point fingers at the innocent. Some of my amazing friends who were not at the party were immediately questioned and attacked. That really got to me. I refused to let innocent people take the blame. I would not let cowardice blanket me in shame. I knew that I needed to do something.

The four of us who didn't plead innocent discussed together how to go about this. And to be honest, the solution was simple: be honest. We did it. We would not stall to admit to our own actions. We directly reported ourselves to the high school administration.

We were four leaders. We were all honor students, athletes and involved in extracurricular activities. The hardest part for me was that a lot of people knew me from many places. I had built a huge social media presence, was involved in the school pep band, and was a student senator. I also, therefore, was the main target for most frustration and anger.

I remember feeling faint the second I admitted it. My chest hurt and felt hollow, and so did my head. I hated disappointing everyone. I hated hurting peoples' feelings. But no matter what, I needed to let everyone know that I did it. I was uncompromising. My ego, my position, my actions at the time were never more valuable than the truth.

In the time immediately after its release, people sent me messages. People threatened me. They called me misogynistic, sexist, f*ckhead, a farce. In the girl's swimming and diving team group chat, someone I didn't even know had called me a "self-proclaimed authoritative dickhead."

Honesty and Making Mistakes

The first thing that I did was tell my mother. I am always going to be honest with her. She obviously thought I was an idiot but trusted that I didn't want to hurt anyone's feelings. She was especially hurt and angry by the texts that were sent to me. She and I decided that the best thing to do was to tell everyone that I am not a sexist or a misogynist, and that they are accusing me for things against my truth and honor; but fighting an uphill battle made things worse.

That was when I realized that nobody gives a shit about your version of the story. Their ideas of what happened are unchanging, already fixated in their minds. To them I had committed the worst crime - we had purposefully made and released a bracket that meticulously rated women based on their bodies for bullying purposes, not a small New Year's thing. Nobody wanted to hear what I have to say. They just wanted to attack me.

Someone anonymously texted me, bringing my mother into the discussion. They claimed that I should forever look at my mother, who would never forgive me, in shame; or that my mother was supporting the growth of a misogynist. That was when I dug my heels into the ground. The worst thing one can do in the Chinese culture is curse one's mother.

I wasn't going to compromise and bend down to be forever labelled as a sexist. I texted people that I came here to tell the truth and nothing but the truth, no matter what other people believed of me. I didn't want to hurt anyone's feelings and I was not doing this to objectify or bully.

As in real life instances, if girls made a bracket of guys, guys would laugh it off. But in my case, I was severely attacked privately via texts and publicly on social media and in message groups.

Two of my friends quietly and publicly apologized but I did not want to give in to toxicity or labelling. But rather than fighting for myself in a constructive way, I took the negative energy of others and made it worse. I felt bad inside, but nobody believed me. I was rude and stubborn in the time following the bracket. My defensive position continued to anger people.

I felt all alone, deserted, even when some of my friends were trying to comfort me. But their efforts were a small voice compared to the storm I faced.

I began to question honesty. Perhaps it was never worth it. Even when people eventually found out about the other three who hid during this whole situation, they never got nearly as angry at them as they did me.

But like I said, a few friends kept me dedicated to honesty. And frankly, they said some of the nicest things to me during that time of my life. My close friend from middle school put it briefly:

This is f*cked up. Look dude, I know you're getting shit for this. Personally, I'm not going to hold a long-term grudge but I know a lot of people are. Owning up to it was the manly thing to do.

And my friend from history class, who was on the bracket, told me this:

Regardless of if there were malicious thought behind it, it is still degrading. I want to feel bad for you because I know you're in a whole world of hurt right now but at the same time I don't... at least you manned up. I know this sucks a lot and even though I'm pissed about it, I went through a lot of shit this week and I know you'll need a friend.

I'm not gonna tell you it's okay and that I'm not upset about it because then I'd be flat out lying. But this will probably be over in about two weeks.

I didn't believe them when they said this would pass, but I, to this day, thank them for being both honest and kind to me when they were both obviously very angry.

When I look back on this incident, I see an ideological movement of anger. I see others angry and I see myself angry. That was when I realized that I needed to change for the future—I needed to make sure that kindness, along with truth, were both uncompromised. I cannot let my own mistakes or the words of others drag me down to rudeness. I needed to keep moving forward and up.

The hardest part for me was that I had to be strong. I had to be willing to fall by honesty. For many months I was the most hated student in my high school. I sent my apology directly to the high school, one which most students or their parents found disingenuine. I lost friends and I lost my seat in the student senate for owning up to my actions. But even when the world around me was against me, I kept trying to improve myself—I made myself that promise.

The bracket was one of the most difficult times in my life. In retrospect, I am glad that it happened. It showed me that I am flawed and can make mistakes. It showed me who was really there for me and who was not when I was in the dumpster. It showed me who was making this situation even more dramatic than it could possibly get. It helped me learn an important lesson: even during fun times with friends, we must be aware of the potential consequences of our actions. No matter how right or "fine" we think we are, we have to develop sensitivities towards others. My friends and I did not think through the consequences of the bracket. If we had been mindful, we could have understood that people can get hurt by it and it should have never been done, let alone posted online. And most importantly, it showed me that I could no longer be content with the common happiness, one of pretentiousness, one of jokes, one of egos, that I was living. I needed to find what happiness and life really meant to me when I would be swimming upstream against society. I choose now to always follow the paradoxical path of truth, kindness, and self-improvement.

I hope you understand that I have changed since the bracket. I am actually close friends with many of the people who most actively were against the bracket. I forgive my friends who did not want to be implicated in the bracket because they each had individual reasons. I forgive those who were mean to me. I became much less arrogant and judgmental of those who messed up around me. Because I finally understand that we are all human beings— teenagers, no less. We mess up sometimes. We all need someone to forgive us and give us another chance. But first and foremost, we must forgive ourselves first and accept the way we are and keep moving forward. I am sorry for having created something that hurt people. I can only hope that you and they may someday forgive me.

I have made mistakes. We have all made mistakes. But mistakes do not give us the excuse to shuffle away reality under a heavy carpet. Being honest was one of the hardest things I've ever had to do. But being honest was also one of the most rewarding things I have ever done. There exists a kind of illumination, purity, solidity that you feel when you are able to stick to your values despite the odds, despite the pressures of the people and oceans and walls around you. I may not understand your values, but my understanding doesn't matter. Likewise, you may not understand mine, but your understanding doesn't matter. When our shield to protect us against the slings and arrows is no longer a mask, but rather our own soul, then may we pass with peace.

I became Juneau when I showed Juneau to the world. I am not a man on a pretentious pedestal. I am just a guy who makes mistakes. But I'm also a guy who owns up to them because the thing that matters most to me is sticking to my values.

In the meantime, I smile without hiding anything. I cry without hiding anything. I can be myself without hiding anything, because I realized that true happiness is the one which waters the growing soul and shows us that we have nothing to hide.

CHAPTER 10

The Pursuit of Happiness

I N HINDUISM, the Trimurti is the Triple deity of supreme divinity. Within the faith, the cosmic functions of creation, maintenance, and destruction are personified as three deities: Brahma, the creator; Vishnu, the preserver; and Shiva, the destroyer.[1] Such is the natural cycle of life. We pray to Brahma for the healthy birth of a newborn. We pray to Vishnu to keep the soil fertile. We pray to Shiva to end disease or illness that causes suffering.

Creation, maintenance, and destruction represent the entirety of the universe. All things are created, all things are maintained, and all things must come to an end. Once we understand this, we begin to understand our own fragile lives and the happiness we can perhaps pursue in context.

One day after school, I was with my English teacher, Mrs. Sharp. She was taking time out of her own Friday to help teach me how to go about the SAT Essay, for which I am very grateful. I could not have performed on the SAT so well without her. In the middle of our conversation, she showed me something she truly believed in and with which she wished more students were familiar: Bloom's Taxonomy.

Bloom's Taxonomy is a hierarchical ordering of cognitive skills that helps both teachers teach and students learn. The revised taxonomy, specifically, focuses on more dynamic application and involves key verbs that apply to each category. In the beginning, when we are all little babies, we start off with learning how to remember. We recognize and recall things. Soon, like the little scientists we are, we learn how to understand. We can explain ideas and concepts with our childlike understanding of the world. Then, we begin to apply. We can execute our own experiments and implement our own functions in new situations. After that, we learn to analyze. We can organize schemata and draw connections between ideas. Then, we evaluate, critiquing and checking information. Finally, we are able to create for ourselves.[2]

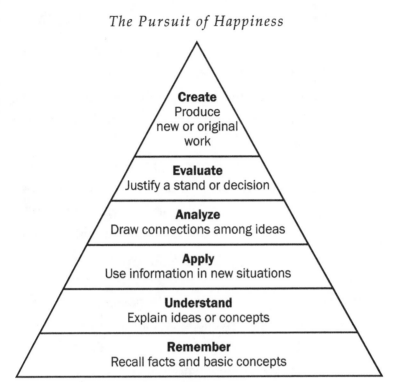

The Pursuit of Happiness

Bloom's Taxonomy

The following example is my own *application* of Bloom's Taxonomy. Let's say that I'm taking a United States history test. I see the name "William Bradford" and *remember* that he is one of the first governors of the Plymouth Colony. Then, I *understand* that he wasn't born here—he arrived in Plymouth because he was on the Mayflower. I begin to *apply* once I realize that other people from that time, like John Winthrop, probably also came to the colonies by boat. I then *analyze*—you see, they were both Puritans, but William Bradford led the Plymouth Colony while John Winthrop led the Massachusetts Bay Colony. I then can *evaluate*—I can defend or refute an argument that the Plymouth Colony had better relations with the Native Americans than the other. Finally, I can *create*—maybe I hypothesize that one of the colonies was more economically successful than the other due to geography.

Now I'm sure you're all confused as to how the Trimurti or Bloom's Taxonomy can help us pursue true happiness. Here's my take. First, happiness is its own "intelligence" and must be learned. Secondly, we can only achieve happiness when we understand the powers of creation and maintenance.

It is easy for us to see and know the power of destruction. In fact, we have total availability bias when it comes to destruction. We mostly see destruction on the news. You can more quickly and more emotionally think of scenarios where planes have crashed than scenarios where planes have landed safely. This is to our biological advantage—as living beings, we need to be wary of destruction so that we may continue to live on and produce offspring. But now, let us see what man can do to itself. Oftentimes, we are destructive. We are destructive to ourselves and destructive to others. For ages, violence, manipulation and corruptness have been the answers to our desires, our wants, our goals. We feel as if sacrifice is necessary. We somehow both fear and commit destruction at the same time. I believe that we humans need to stop destroying. That is for the universe to naturally do. However, we can only realize such when we understand the true powers of creation and maintenance.

According to the Second Law of Thermodynamics, entropy naturally increases. Order becomes disorder. Complex proteins break down into smaller molecules. But if everything turns to chaos… then how do biological beings stay alive? We take and expend energy from the universe. We consume energy stored in the bonds of the molecules of food to create new cells and maintain old ones. And when destruction occurs or must occur, it is the universe's doing. Correct, apoptosis, or self-induced cell death, is a very common biological action to stop mutant or nonfunctional or infected cells from replicating. But we have no control over whether or not a cell will develop with functional problems.

I believe humans are one of the greatest collective sources of destruction and chaos. Optimistically, we are also one of the greatest collective sources of creation and order. But we find destruction so much easier to do. Sure, some of it is thermodynamics. But is egging someone's house really "thermodynamics"? I believe we will never understand the consequences of destruction until we understand the power of creation.

Only a small percentage of people are self-actualized. Only a small percentage of people develop postconventional morality. And I believe only a small percentage of people truly value creation.

Valuing creation isn't as simple as following orders. Valuing creation is a mindfulness that can only come from within. A lot of people like to meditate in the morning before they go to work. They feel it makes them happier and more fulfilled, and it probably does. But then they go to work and completely forget about mindfulness. They lose a lot of happiness throughout the day due to inconveniences, frustrations, and the fact of just being at work. Mindfulness is not something you just forever achieve if you say "ohm" for five minutes in the morning; mindfulness is an active process that requires dedication (also known as maintenance). And along with valuing creation comes gratitude.

My parents taught me basic table manners, but I took them to the next level. I have a habit of saying "please" and "thank you" and "sorry" more than most people are comfortable with. But I won't ever stop. I am grateful for what the world has blessed me with. I constantly looked for good things when I was younger and appreciated them for what they were. I was blessed when I was cleared to swim at the Eastern Zones, despite my wounded knee. I was blessed when I was forgiven by some of my close friends after the bracket, despite the harsh words also thrown at me. I was blessed when my psychology teacher let me finish my test, despite the harsh words I threw at him when he first tried to take my exam away. And to this day I thank the Lord and my mother for every time my mother cooks a nice meal for me. We need to count our blessings every single living day. And once I started looking for and feeling my blessings, even if they were in disguise, I felt closer to the universe, and more blessings started coming to me.

Now, this brings me to my next part. After you graciously value and appreciate creation and what the universe gives us, you begin to realize that most anything can also be created by you. That includes intelligence, self-confidence, self-love, and happiness. But at the same time, most anything can also be destroyed by you. That is the balance of yin and yang. We must constantly understand our powers and use both the dark and the light for good.

Happiness is its own form of an intelligence. It requires learning how to accept the humongous pits of bad and continue to smile at even the smallest grain of good. And it goes directly in opposition with a tricky word: "deserving."

I'm going to be real: life can be disappointing. At one time or another, your friends will disappoint you; your family will disappoint you, and everything sucks. But you see, everything will disappoint you if and only if you do not have the right expectations.

I expected my best friend to introduce me to his new friends. He didn't. That expectation caused me to be angry, sad, and obnoxious at him. What if I just didn't expect such at all? I would have probably been happy and blessed.

I expected my mom to not forget gardening tools on the floor of the garage behind my car so I wouldn't run over them and accidentally pop a tire. But she did. Obviously, that made me angry, but it made me realize that no one is perfect. Neither am I. So, I can't judge them or be enraged. My mom is the best mom ever and I love her. But I don't expect anyone to be perfect, because that will surely disappoint. Knowing that people are imperfect yet still loving them makes us true human beings.

Deserving has always been a harsh word to me because it reminds me of overbearing expectations with an attitude of ingratitude. We need to use it carefully. If someone worked hard and did comparatively best at a swim meet, then they deserve to win overall first place. But we do not simply deserve things without work. In my mind, we naturally "deserve" three things: life, liberty, and the pursuit of happiness. Beyond that is for you to find a blessing.

Some feel that they deserve to be treated well by strangers.

Some say that they deserve respect.

I am not quite sure about these assumptions. The word "deserving" may be dangerous because it gives us the assumption that we can just sit on our asses and wait for people to hand us platters of food. I think other than the fundamental three things, life, liberty, and the pursuit of happiness, we have to consider working for the things we wish for, such as respect, kindness, abundance, and power. Everything made in this world is everything worked for. I learned happiness from pursuing happiness, from understanding independence and self-love, positive energy and the positive truth, the blessing of blessings, and the power of creation and maintenance.

My mother, brother, and I were driving to Boston and had the opportunity to try out Chick-fil-A by a highway exit in Massachusetts. My mother was immediately bothered that there was a long line. But I was not. I realized that we're not in a rush to get to Boston. We're blessed to get to try out Chick-fil-A. And I openly told her, "at least we'll have more time to think about what we want to order." Sometimes the only way to make a situation good or feel blessed is with humor, and that humor can help you see the brighter side of things. And thank goodness we did have more time to think about everything we wanted to order, because Chick-fil-A has some amazing stuff, man.

I started dieting a few weeks before we went to Boston. Not a "starving" diet, just calorie control to burn fat and gain muscle. That inadvertently led me to be more mindful of what I was eating and be even more grateful for the delicious things I get to have. Right before typing this, I had delicious, home-grown green peppers and that was like dessert for me. Anyway, I ordered the cobb salad at Chick-fil-A. The salad was humongous, with lettuce, cheese, grape tomatoes, bacon, sliced hard-boiled egg, fried chicken, and this amazing avocado lime ranch dressing, and these delicious charred tomato crispy red bell peppers which easily were healthier and tastier than croutons. I highly recommend it! That was one of the best blessings I have ever tasted. And if you are able to talk about something special with as much passion or joy or mindfulness as a teenage boy talking about a cobb salad, then you are on the right path to happiness.

I want to touch on a few more things. I do see some valid points in existentialism. Existentialism claims that our existence is pointless, and that we are insignificant. The emptiness and meaninglessness of life truly terrifies us, which is why we create artificial structures such as school, work, and the economy. I'm not sure if there is a true meaning to life. But since we cannot prove it meaningless, I suggest we humans always have hope. We need to encourage everyone around us to always have hope. Hope is not a strategy; it is the single most important motivation towards finding better. If you want to live a better life, then you need to constantly be positive in the face of the dark void. I personally think life's lack of meaning makes it beautiful. Because then, life is a clean slate. Therefore, life is what YOU make of it. You can do anything and everything you want.

We must never cease to make the most or to pursue the best. A lot of people do not want to make choices for themselves or take risks or go for what they want or do anything in life. But the biggest relief is that first jump and the first "Geronimo!" We need to get out there, use what we have, and seek something greater. We can be happy and never settle to make ourselves happier.

Part of making the most is understanding when to "regret." Regretting is a negative condemnation of our past selves. We cannot simply shut away our pasts like that; we must accept what has happened and learn from it. Weaker people simply regret their past actions and go on with their lives. Stronger people accept their past actions and learn from them. In line with that, never feel like you are missing out on anything. We need to be happy with the choices we make. Some nights I go out and have fun with my friends—no regrets. Some nights I decide to stay in and write a book, apparently—no regrets. Nobody else can tell you what you value; you need to identify what you care about and stick to pursuing those things.

In addition to making the most, money should never be the center of your mind. Once you put money in the center of your mind, a few things happen. First, you begin to look at everything like a transaction and you regress to preconventional morality. Secondly, your accomplishments on the hierarchy of needs fall back to worrying about the basics. In other words, when money is all you think about, you can never be self-actualized, and you can never achieve postconventional morality. You will lose sight of happiness, joy, and universal ethics. I know there are tight crunches when you don't have money. But we cannot let worry or fear or money dominate our minds. We need to make the most of what we have. My mother's side in the beginning was very poor, but they still came together like a family and enjoyed what they could—a nice family dinner. And I am grateful and blessed that my mother showed me, no matter what financial situation we're in, that we can enjoy life.

Penultimately, social connections are extremely important for your happiness. I had the pleasure and the absolute blessing of watching Harvard Psychologist Daniel Gilbert give a presentation at Harvard Medical School. A famed TED Talk presenter and author of *Stumbling on Happiness*, he has dedicated most of his research to finding out what exactly is happiness to us humans. And his quote on social connections says it all:

If I wanted to predict your happiness, and I could know only one thing about you, I wouldn't want to know your gender, religion, health, or income. I'd want to know about your social network—about your friends and family and the strength of your bonds with them.[3]

My great-grandparents were not worried about money. They were concerned about family, about friends. We need to allow ourselves to be healthily connected with people who shine light on our lives. I believe both extroverts and introverts would benefit from some extremely strong and intimate bonds. The world we create is a cooperation. We need to constructively share our thoughts, feelings, and beliefs with each other in order to progress as a society. Although octopuses may be just as smart as us, they are not social creatures. Imagine how the world would look today if they started socializing before we humans did…

Finally, I would like to talk about the cover of this book. Friends are amazing and can help lift us up. They inspire us to be more. And while life is beautiful with them, we need to realize that life can still be beautiful when we're alone. The original painting, *Wanderer above the Sea of Fog*, shows us both conquest over the earth yet also the smallness of man, who is on his new journey into the unknown.[4] We can gaze at this beautiful universe and at the same time be staring into our own reflecting souls. And we must stand for ourselves no matter the circumstance, looking to the future with bright yet aged eyes. But never forget to pat yourself on the back.

This is just the perspective of a teenage boy. I think I've said what I need to. I'm going to go hang out with my friends and then take a nap.

Caspar David Friedrich: *Wanderer above the Sea of Fog*.
Collection of Hamburger Kunsthalle, Hamburg.

SHORT STORY

I WROTE MANY SHORT STORIES in eighth grade. Back then, it was my dream to one day publish them as a collection. That has not yet happened, but for the time being I would like to end this book with my favorite piece. Please enjoy "The Reef," unedited and unabridged.

The Reef

May 10ᵗʰ, 2016

They were two different of the same.

Never 'til the world ended would they part.

Friendship is a beautiful thing, and even more beautiful in its genuine.

Long ago, two orphans found each other and assisted each other in survival. They were the Porpoise and the Seagull.

The Porpoise and the Seagull were two peas in a pod. Two "brothers from another mother." They threw away their inherent differences and only focused on their friendship. Need not matter, fin nor wing, together they let go of judgement and only saw the light in each other. They worked together to achieve any supper or prank they desired.

The sun rose above the horizon. Its orange and red streaks flew across the sky. The water glimmered below it, almost as if in response. The waters flowed and waved silently below the painted sky.

The now grown Porpoise arose from his sleep. He slowly moved his tail back and forth and headed towards the bay. There lay hundreds of resting ships, carrying many birds on their masts. As if in acknowledgement of the white Porpoise's presence, the Seagull swiftly dove down towards him.

They didn't speak nor even say a word. They both knew what was important—to eat and to prank. They felt comfortable with one another. Their connection ran deeper than the bottom of the deepest ravine.

They lay themselves in the warm sun. The clouds climbed across the now blue sky. The breeze gently hugged the rolling waves. The buoy bells rang and the other birds began to sing their songs. Harmony protruded through the air, harmony of community and love.

The Porpoise and the Seagull went outwards from the shore to the nearby schools of fish. They jumped around and swung up and down in the sea and in the air. Water swooshed and splashed all around. They played tag and chased the small fish.

Then, something happened. All of the fish randomly scattered and shouted, blinding the Porpoise's vision. When he was finally able to see again, he was alone. He quickly checked for the Seagull, but couldn't find him. The Porpoise called for him and, in the far distance, a muffled cry replied. A barracuda had snatched the Seagull and bit down on him. Blood and screams spread throughout the ocean. The Porpoise cried for the Seagull. He began to pursue the barracuda. The Porpoise pushed through the kelp forests, shoving all slow fish aside. He breathed heavily and followed the barracuda's tail. He turned left and right, up and down. But then, the Porpoise got tangled in a stray net. The Porpoise used all his willpower to keep pushing ahead and tried to catch up to the barracuda, but the sly fish smirked and swayed downwards into the abyss.

He had taken his friend. His only friend. Emptiness filled the Porpoise. But, that emptiness soon dissipated, for a new feeling was inside his gut…

Revenge.

Later that night, the small moon barely shown. The dark clouds consumed the sky and only the lighthouse's luminescence pierced the quiet night.

The Porpoise knew what he had to do. He kept swimming until he reached the cave of the barracudas. Then, he silently crept towards them. But, as if time stopped, he saw the dead body of the Seagull. Bruises and bumps engulfed the once beautifully feathered skin and limbs were torn off, blood oozing from the floating parts. In the Seagull's eyes the Porpoise could see his friend's last moments of suffering and terror. And the anger in the Porpoise was overwhelming.

The Porpoise swam silently towards the three sleeping barracudas and quickly struck. The Porpoise, engulfed in rage bit the closest barracuda's neck—the one that murdered his friend—and jerked the barracuda's head around. The barracuda's skull soon snapped in half as a lifeless scream of agony filled the room. The other two barracuda swiftly tried to attack the Porpoise. They struck him first in the face, stunning him. The Porpoise could feel blood trickling down his cheek. The two planned for a final blow, but the pain and sadness in the Porpoise made him faster. He quickly scooped up both of their bodies in his mouth and snapped both of them in half. The narrow and damp cave was quickly removed of water and, in its place, blood filled the dark lair. And only the Porpoise left from the cave.

The sun now shone again, this time much more sadly. Its yellow glow was underwhelming as it barely colored the sky. The sky bloomed a darker blue. It was as if the entire universe felt the disturbance in the balance of life.

The Porpoise, full of satisfaction, swam up to the surface. And in his reflection, he expected to see himself. But when he gazed upon his reflection, he only saw a murderer unrecognizable. A humungous bloody scar ran down his face and in his eyes were the sins of demons. A glowing fire erupted around him and he no longer knew who he was, who he once was, or who he would ever be.

The sight of his killing self destroyed his soul, and he slowly closed his eyes. He had done wrong. And instead of saving the Seagull, he killed three more in the process. He wanted to die.

He rested in the middle of the sea, waiting to arrive to the eternal hell he was bound to be sent to, but instead, he felt a whirlpool beneath his tail. It swooshed and swayed and engulfed him until he could no longer see.

Was he finally to his damnation?

After what felt like a million years, he was able to feel again. He quickly opened his eyes and his sight slowly restored. But in this place was nothing he recognized. Whole new forests, whole new fish, whole new seas.

The same sun now shone in its beautiful purples and oranges, barely rising above the surface. The waters twinkled and were alive. Schools of red, yellow, green fish lively flew past him.

Why was this hell so... *nice*?

And just as the question emitted in his head, it omitted. Bright lights spontaneously flashed in his eyes until his vision was yet again blinded. But in its place he saw some creature he had never seen before. It seemed to have the tail of the most majestical fish with gleaming and glittering scales. But with it were the torso and head and arms of a... human?

The Porpoise asked in its mind, what did the thing want? And immediately the angel replied. For the mermaid showed the Porpoise flashing pictures of a dark and dead coral reef. The souls of ghostly fish roamed the mortifying sea and to the Porpoise stood out one soul—the soul of the Seagull, his Seagull.

He would do anything to get his friend back. And the mermaid answered again. For the only way the Porpoise could get his friend's soul would be to save everyone else's souls—even the barracudas. But, the Seagull would never remember his dear friend ever again.

The Porpoise knew that it was the right thing to do, it was unjust the Seagull was taken away. The Porpoise loved the Seagull. The Porpoise demanded a promise that the Seagull would never be attacked again. But with that came an extra price.

The mermaid said that such a bargain would come with a big responsibility—the Porpoise must present his soul to the dead waters and *become* the coral reef. He would need to give up his Porpoise body in order to revive the Seagull.

And the guilt washed over him. For the Porpoise had also killed the three barracudas, and he knew that they should have lived their lives, too, no matter how evil he thought they were. And with this, he could restore the lives of all the unjustly killed fish *and* the brittle coral reef.

And the Porpoise quickly agreed to the deal. And as he agreed the bright lights dimmed away and so did the mermaid. In his vision returned the reef where he had originally been sent to after the whirlpool.

Although the Porpoise was never told the direction of the Dead Waters, he immediately knew and felt and sensed where they were. He knew what he had to do. He hastily swam as fast as he could, for miles on end. He passed hundreds of forests, hundreds of live reefs and never stopped once for a break. His will pushed him towards the Dead Waters.

Sunrises and sunsets passed on his journey. Storms and winds and calms all swept through the oceans and back. The Porpoise felt as if he could see the colors and pains of the water. He saw the shining moon again and again, each day changing its dress. And beaches of many sands passed by his venture.

And he had found it. The Dead Waters.

He saw all of the lifeless souls, moaning and crying, not knowing who they were or what they once were. That was the pain of death. And he saw the Seagull. His tepid emotion stuck on his face and tears welled into the Porpoise's eyes.

The Porpoise opened his heart, not just to the Seagull, but to the barracudas, the waters, the stars, and the coral reef and he felt the kisses.

The Seagull woke up from his slumber. And it was that time of year again. He would venture to the Great Barrier Reef. He spread his wings and soared for days on end. Why he traveled to the reef, he did not know. But he felt happiness and comfort at the reef. There was an inherent warmth and life to the Great Barrier Reef.

He reached the coral reef and soared, circling it in the sky. Little did he know that below him stood tall and proud his first and only friend. And without ever knowing, the Seagull made a promise to the Great Barrier Reef.

That until the world ended, they would not part.

NOTES

Chapter 1

1. Sigmund Freud et al., *The Standard Edition of the Complete Psychological Works of Sigmund Freud*, 24 vols. (New York, NY: Macmillan, 1974).

2. John B. Watson, *Behaviorism* (Piscataway, NJ: Transaction Publishers, 1998).

3. Abraham H. Maslow, *Towards a Psychology of Being*, 2nd ed. (New York, NY: D. Van Nostrand, 1968).

4. Abraham H. Maslow, "A Theory of Human Motivation," *Psychological Review* 50, no. 4 (1943): doi:10.1037/h0054346.

5. Vincent Van Gogh, *Bedroom in Arles*, 1888, Musée D'Orsay, Paris.

6. *Buddhist Monk Budai*, The Metropolitan Museum of Art, New York.

Chapter 2

1. Edward Hoffman, *The Right to Be Human: A Biography of Abraham Maslow* (New York, NY: St. Martin's Press, 1988).

2. Portal 2, computer software, 2011.

3. Ellen J. Langer, *Mindfulness* (Reading, MA: Addison-Wesley, 1989).

4. Sigmund Freud et al., "Beyond the Pleasure Principle," in *The Standard Edition of the Complete Psychological Works of Sigmund Freud*, vol. 18 (New York, NY: Macmillan, 1920).

5. Sigmund Freud et al., "The Ego and the Id," in *The Standard Edition of the Complete Psychological Works of Sigmund Freud*, vol. 19 (New York, NY: Macmillan, 1920).

6. Anna Freud, *The Ego and the Mechanisms of Defense* (London: Hogarth Press and the Institute of Psychoanalysis, 1937).

7. Elaine Hatfield, John T. Cacioppo, and Richard L. Rapson, "Emotional Contagion," *Review of Personality and Social Psychology* 14 (1992).

8. Richard D. Lane, "Neural Correlates of Conscious Emotional Experience," *Series in Affective Science: Cognitive Neuroscience of Emotion* (New York, NY: Oxford University Press, 2000).

9. Anthony C. Little, Benedict C. Jones, and Lisa M. DeBruine, "Facial Attractiveness: Evolutionary Based Research," *Philosophical Transactions of the Royal Society B: Biological Sciences* 366, no. 1571 (2011): doi:10.1098/rstb.2010.0404.

10. Ronald E. Riggio and Sarah Stevenson, "There's Magic in Your Smile: How Smiling Affects Your Brain,"

Psychology   Today,   June   25,   2012, https://www.psychologytoday.com/us/blog/cutting-edge-leadership/201206/there-s-magic-in-your-smile.

11. *Shrek,* dir. Andrew Adamson and Vicky Jenson, by Ted Elliot, Terry Rossio, Joe Stillman, and Roger S. H. Schulman, perf. Mike Meyers, Eddie Murphy, and Cameron Diaz, 2001.

12. Albert Bandura, "The Self System in Reciprocal Determinism.," *American Psychologist* 33, no. 4 (1978): doi:10.1037//0003-066x.33.4.344.

Chapter 3

1. Edwin G. Boring and Carl Murchison, *A History of Psychology in Autobiography* (Worcester, MA: Clark University Press, 1930).

2. "Pioneers In Our Field: Jean Piaget - Champion of Children's Ideas," *Scholastic,* n.d., https://www.scholastic.com/teachers/articles/teaching-content/pioneers-our-field-jean-piaget-champion-childrens-ideas/.

3. Jean Piaget, Howard E. Gruber, and J. Jacques Vonèche, *The Essential Piaget* (Northvale, NJ: J. Aronson, 1995).

4. Hermann Ebbinghaus, *Über Das Gedächtnis* (Leipzig: Duncker & Humblot, 1885).

5. Patrick Finan, "The Effects of Sleep Deprivation," n.d., https://www.hopkinsmedicine.org/health/wellness-and-prevention/the-effects-of-sleep-deprivation.

6. Habib Yaribeygi, Yunes Panahi, Hedayat Sahraei, Thomas P. Johnston, and Amirhossein Sahebkar, "The Impact of Stress on Body Function: A Review," *Experimental and Clinical Sciences Journal* 16 (2017): doi:10.17179/excli2017-480.

7. *Kung Fu Panda 3*, dir. Jennifer Y. Nelson and Alessandro Carloni, by Jonathan Aibel, and Glenn Berger, perf. Jack Black, Bryan Cranston, Dustin Hoffman, and Angelina Jolie, 2016.

8. Robert M. Yerkes and John D. Dodson, "The Relation of Strength of Stimulus to Rapidity of Habit-Formation," *Journal of Comparative Neurology and Psychology* 18, no. 5 (1908): 459–482, doi:10.1002/cne.920180503.

9. Donald O. Hebb, "Drives and the C.N.S. (Conceptual Nervous System)," *Psychological Review* 62, no. 4 (1955): 243–254, doi:10.1037/h0041823.

Chapter 4

1. *Merriam-Webster Dictionary*, Collegiate 11th ed., s.v. "independence."

2. *Merriam-Webster Dictionary*, Collegiate 11th ed., s.v. "independent."

3. Lisa S. Blackwell, Kali H. Trzesniewski, and Carol S. Dweck, "Implicit Theories of Intelligence Predict Achievement across an Adolescent Transition: a Longitudinal Study and an Intervention," *Child*

Development 78, no. 1 (2007): 246–263, doi:10.1111/j.1467-8624.2007.00995.x.

4. Brooke Donald, "Willpower Is in Your Mind, Not in a Sugar Cube, Say Stanford Scholars," August 27, 2013, https://news.stanford.edu/news/2013/august/willpower-study-sugar-082713.html.

5. Lawrence Kohlberg, "The Development of Modes of Thinking and Choices in Years 10 to 16," PhD diss., (University of Chicago, 1958).

6. *The Office*, on NBC.

7. *Barnyard*, dir. Steve Oedekerk, by Steve Oedekerk, perf. Kevin James, Courtney Cox, and Sam Elliott, 2006.

8. Algernon Sidney, *Discourses Concerning Government* (London: Booksellers of London and Westminster, 1698).

9. Benjamin Franklin and Richard Saunders, *Poor Richard's Almanack* (New York, NY: Barse & Hopkins, 1736).

Chapter 5

1. "So They Say!," *Owosso Argus-Press* (Owosso, MI), Apr. 2, 1935

2. *The Reader's Digest*, September 1940, 84.

3. Ben Dattner, "Preventing 'Groupthink,'" *Psychology Today*, April 20, 2011, https://www.psychologytoday.com/us/blog/credit-and-blame-work/201104/preventing-groupthink.

4. Robert J. Sternberg, "Triangulating Love," in *The Altruism Reader: Selections from Writings on Love, Religion, and Science*, ed. Thomas J. Oord (West Conshohocken, PA: Templeton Foundation, 2007), 332.

5. Robert J. Sternberg, *Cupid's Arrow: The Course of Love through Time* (Cambridge: Cambridge University Press, 1998).

Entr'acte

1. *Bao*, dir. Domee Shi, 2018.

Chapter 6

1. Alexander Thomas and Stella Chess, *Temperament and Development* (New York, NY: Brunner/Mazel, 1977).

2. Mary D. Ainsworth, "Patterns of Attachment," *Clinical Psychologist* 38, no. 2 (1985): pp. 27-29, doi:10.1037/e550432011-004.

3. Judith Solomon, Carol George, and Annemieke De Jong, "Children Classified as Controlling at Age Six: Evidence of Disorganized Representational Strategies and Aggression at Home and at School," *Development and Psychopathology* 7, no. 3 (1995): pp. 447-463, doi:10.1017/s0954579400006623.

4. Mary Main and Judith Solomon, "Procedures for Identifying Infants as Disorganized/Disoriented during the Ainsworth Strange Situation," in *Attachment in the Preschool Years: Theory, Research, and Intervention*, eds. Mark T. Greenberg, Dante Cicchetti, and E. Mark

Cummings, 121-160 (Chicago, IL: University of Chicago Press, 1993).

5. Mary Main and Erik Hesse, "Parents' Unresolved Traumatic Experiences Are Related to Infant Disorganized Attachment Status: Is Frightened and/or Frightening Parental Behavior the Linking Mechanism?," in *Attachment in the Preschool Years: Theory, Research, and Intervention*, eds. Mark T. Greenberg, Dante Cicchetti, and E. Mark Cummings, 161-184 (Chicago, IL: University of Chicago Press, 1993).

6. J. K. Rowling and Mary K. GrandPré, *Harry Potter and the Sorcerer's Stone* (Thorndike, ME: Thorndike Press, 2003).

7. John Singleton Copley, *Watson and the Shark*, 1778, National Gallery of Art, Washington, D.C.

8. "Pawn Stars: Stacks of Pristine 10 Charizard Pokemon Cards (Season 14) | History," YouTube video, "Pawn Stars," November 13, 2017, https://www.youtube.com/watch?v=iIRedvXGmYo.

9. *Un Padre No Tan Padre*, dir. Raúl Martínez Resendez, by Alberto Bremer, perf. Héctor Bonilla, Benny Ibarra de Llano, Jacqueline Bracamontes, Arturo Barba, and Sergio Mayer Mori, 2016.

Chapter 7

1. Hillary Anger Elfenbein and Nalini Ambady, "On the Universality and Cultural Specificity of Emotion

Recognition: A Meta-Analysis.," *Psychological Bulletin* 128, no. 2 (2002): pp. 203-235, doi:10.1037//0033-2909.128.2.203.

2. Bennett Cerf, *Shake Well Before Using: a New Collection of Impressions and Anecdotes, Mostly Humorous* (London: Hammond, 1951).

3. Anais Nin, *Henry and June* (London: Penguin Books, 2001).

4. Wang Dawei, *Women Hold up Half the Sky, They Force Mountains and Rivers to Change Colors*, 1975, Liaoning Cultural Center, https://hdl.handle.net/10622/32CF61F2-AFF8-4EF3-BE16-506B633DE306.

5. Rembrandt Van Rijn, *The Storm on the Sea of Galilee*, 1633, Isabella Stewart Gardner Museum, Boston; Stolen in 1990.

Chapter 8

1. George Frederic Watts, *Hope*, 1886, Tate Britain, London.

Chapter 9

Chapter 9 incorporates no outside sources

Chapter 10

1. Zimmer, Heinrich Robert Zimmer and Joseph Campbell, *Myths and Symbols in Indian Art and Civilization* (Princeton, NJ: Princeton University Press, 2017).

2. David Krathwohl et al., *A Taxonomy for Learning, Teaching, and Assessing: a Revision of Bloom's Taxonomy of Educational Objectives* (New York, NY: Longman, 2001).

3. "The Science Behind the Smile," Harvard Business Review (Harvard Business Publishing, October 8, 2014), https://hbr.org/2012/01/the-science-behind-the-smile.

4. Caspar David Friedrich, *Wanderer above the Sea of Fog*, 1818, Hamburger Kunsthalle, Hamburg.